"*Severed Soul* is the powerful, life-changing story of one woman's incredible journey through the deep, dark valley of despair and betrayal, and God's amazing faithfulness to deliver and heal her against all odds. I was gripped by the trauma she had to endure and inspired by her faith to keep on going and never give up. This is a great read for all people of faith."

—Rev. Paul Burton, associate pastor, Tremont Temple Baptist Church

"*Severed Soul* offers insight and perspective that would help pastors and laypersons better serve persons who have suffered trauma. This is a thoughtful work that will challenge perceptions within the Church, but I believe it will help bring the reality of God into the reality of broken lives."

—Christopher Brown, pastor

"*Severed Soul* is a book of trauma, determination, despair and pure revelation. This book will open your eyes as well as fill your heart with the author's amazing story-telling style, and contains excellent information on and resources about PTSD, told in a way that you can relate to no matter what your trauma. I couldn't stop reading and I have my fingers crossed that there will be a sequel."

—Monique Houde, author of
Blinded by Lov

"*Severed Soul* reaches into the despair of abuse. Sadly, there are wounded souls that suffer from such tragedy on a daily basis. For a book like this to be written is a call for repair in the hearts of those who search for help."

—D. Dodge, writer, director,
J.L. One Productions

"Read this book and conquer your fears."

—William May, chief of police (retired)

"This book is unlike anything that I have ever read. I believe that it is incumbent upon those in healthcare to recognize that the damage done to the soul and psyche by Post-traumatic Stress Disorder and verbally abusive living situations can create deep scars not easily seen or recognized by the human eye."

—Joyce Carroll Fletcher, RN, MSN

SEVERED
SOUL

One Woman's Journey Through
Post Traumatic Stress

Dear Soldier,
II TIMOTHY 1 v 7
Thank you for your
service. Always keep
the faith.
    Love & Blessings
        Janice
        JRVallee

SEVERED SOUL

One Woman's Journey Through
Post Traumatic Stress

———

J.L. Vallee

Westminster Info Press

Requests and further information, contact the author:
JLVallee@severedsoul.com

Westminster Info Press (WIP)
PO Box 62
Westminster, MA 01473

Book design by:
Arbor Books, Inc.
19 Spear Road, Suite 301
Ramsey, NJ 07446
www.arborbooks.com

Printed in the United States of America

Severed Soul
J.L. Vallee
1. Title 2. Author 3. Memoir

Library of Congress Control Number: 2007939226

ISBN 10: 0-9800810-0-9
ISBN 13: 978-0-9800810-0-8

DEDICATION

My Faith

My Children

My Parents, brothers and my extended family

Mish & Family... I love you

To all my Sista's, Karla, Geri, Monique, Lisa, Karen, Shauna
Janet, Donna, Laura, Shelia, Sarah, Dianna, Judy, Debbie,
Jan, Joan, Lynn, Rana, Latrice, Jean, Sally

Pastor Alex

My Church Family

Ron Burton Training Village; for nurturing my boys
The Burton Family for their loving Faith and Mama Smith

Battered Woman's Resources

The Vietnam Veterans of America Chapters

Veterans Outreach Centers

In memory of Memere, Pepere & Janette Howard

To All those who have had trauma

TABLE of CONTENTS

INTRODUCTION

I always thought Post Traumatic Stress Disorder is a veteran thing, they deal with that; a causality of war. Never did I realize—what that causality was, until I was diagnosed with the same "thing."

I hope as you read my story, you can feel my fear, my shock, my devastation and pain of an ordinary woman, who lives through unordinary circumstances. And that you come to an understanding that Post Traumatic Stress Disorder is not just a veteran "thing." It is a human thing.

We all do need to be familiar with, Post Traumatic Stress because it does not mean you are crazy. Those who have lived through a life altering situation are all "wounded human beings."

"For God hath not given us the spirit of fear; but of power, and of love, and of a sound mind."

—II Timothy 1: 7

CHAPTER 1
THE PARTY BUS

What a beautiful, sunny, warm, and exciting day this was supposed to be. Little did I know it would be my worst nightmare.

My husband of fourteen years, Eddie, and I arrived at the local Staples parking lot. The party bus was being loaded with coolers, chairs, and barbeque grills. The sounds of chatter and anticipation were all around us. As we climbed on the big party bus, we were on our way to see a Jimmy Buffett show. The bus was chartered by a local business- man named Arthur, and his wife, Jane. Most of the partygoers were local fireman, business owners, veterinarians, and friends of Arthur. There was also a couple named Bill and Patty. Bill worked with Eddie at the fire department; they spent a lot of time together at the firehouse and also tipped beers at local pubs. Patty and Jane were good friends. They all knew each other well. I was relatively new to this group of people; as I climbed on the

1

bus and sat down I felt a little out of place. Eddie was a call fireman; whenever the city had an emergency, off he would go. He recently was accepted to become a full-time fireman. So this was all fairly new to me and so were these people.

I had prepared for this day for weeks. I had gone to the mall and bought Eddie a Hawaiian shirt especially for the concert. My friend Dianna had gone shopping with me at Macy's, where we found the cutest pair of capri pants; they were a beautiful turquoise color with parrots all over them. They were so awesome; I called Patty and told her about them and where to buy them. Patty and Jane each bought a pair in different colors also. We were dressed perfectly to go to a Jimmy Buffet show. I reminisced quite a bit about going to this show. I have been a fan of Jimmy Buffett for many years. I had last seen him in Arizona twenty-four years ago at the ASU Activity Center on March 9, 1979. He put on a good show and sang all his sing-along songs the price of a ticket then was $7.50. I still have the concert ticket. Imagine that!

When I think of Jimmy, I think of Jerry Jeff Walker; they are good friends. Jerry Jeff was always my favorite. His book *Gypsy Songman* is a classic read. He has stories of he and Jimmy having a whopping good run in the Florida Keys. I have personally meet Jerry Jeff and his band many times. I can say this much—they sure can get a crowd to sing along with them and the "Mr. Bojangles" tune has never sounded so good by anyone but him.

Jerry Jeff, over the years, has always touched my life with his music, since I had been a rowdy twenty-something up until my present jazzy forty-something. Once I even donated BOSE speakers to his music school in Austin, Texas, for a fundraiser. Jerry and his wife, Susan, have been developing a school for aspiring musicians in Austin. I had spent my younger years in Arizona; I knew many people in the music industry back then.

Oh, those were the days. We used to have bands set up in our backyards and do an all weekend sing-along and dream about standing on a corner in Winslow, Arizona. We drank a little beer and had some fun, nothing bad; it was always about the music.

So, here I am riding on a bus to see Jimmy Buffett. How cool is that! It has been a long time. We all looked like we were going to the Keys dressed in the garb that makes Margaritaville famous. The host, Arthur, started passing out beers to all. Then out came the Jell-O shots; he had them served up on a big tray. I knew better; I cannot handle hard liquor nor did I want to become oblivious to my surroundings. I wanted to see Jimmy Buffett sing and have my sing-along, sober. Or somewhat, anyway, I thought. So I nursed a nice cold Corona beer. Lately, I had not wanted to drink too much alcohol. Over the years I masked my pain with alcohol, but lately I did not really care for it. It is just not worth the pain and suffering of hangovers and regrets. Plus, I am allergic to the poison. Seems like my inner spirit or maturity was mysteriously leading me, telling me things were changing in my life. Or was it the change of life, or "pre-mental pause," as I call it? All I know is I was changing.

The people on the bus grew louder with eagerness to get to our destination. Upon arrival everyone sprang into action, as on a movie set. I could hear the loud bangs and feel the jolts of the bottom storage compartments opening up under the bus. As I walked out of the bus, I was amazed to see the busyness of setting up this camp behind the bus. I grabbed my chairs from the storage bins; the chairs were

made like the American Flag and they represented support
for September 11th. They were the most comfortable chairs;
I had bought them on a business trip in Oshkosh, Wisconsin,
while I worked for BOSE Corporation. They were different
than most, made larger and stronger than normal. I had
them shipped back on the BOSE truck; all my coworkers on
that trip brought some back, too. September 11th was a day
I will never forget as long as I live. My heart aches for all the
people lost and the attack on our country. I cried from that
devastation. We lost trust of being free from harm that day.
The trauma surely hit home. I had never seen anything like
the magnitude of this camp as I set up my chairs. There was
hardly anywhere to put them. There were so many people
and stuff everywhere—tables, grills, chairs, you name it. This
was not going to be a sing-along tailgate party. But I could
feel something was out of control.

The coolers lined the back of both sides of the bus. Eddie
was hovering with Bill; he asked me what I wanted to drink.
I looked in the coolers. I had never seen so much booze at
a private venue in all my life. I thought to myself, I just want
to relax, put my feet up, and have a glass of wine. But that
was not happening. Most people on the bus had a good buzz
going. There was music playing very loudly from the bus
next to us. There was a DJ; I could not believe it, a DJ in a
parking lot. You could barely speak to one another; there was
lots of noise. The bus next to us was a corporate-sponsored
Rum Bus. The grills they had were huge. It was like a full
restaurant/pub setup. It was unbelievable! People were getting louder and louder. Everyone was dancing in the dirt,
feeling no pain.

A group of us decided to walk around and see all the
buses and just check things out. Well, it was like Mardi

Gras: beads and boobs. Eddie bought me a strand of beads I wanted; we had matching ones—it was so sweet. The necklace was strung with parrots and custom-type beads. I put them on; they kind of matched my capris.

But I had seen enough! We went back to our camp. When we got back, crowds had gathered near our bus and the Rum Bus. There was going to be a wet T-shirt contest. Well, I wanted no part of that. To my amazement, all the women on my bus wanted to enter. But I was sober and they were not. It all happened so fast. The women went on the bus and put the Rum T-shirts on. They were tying knots in the material to hold their boobs up. Men were painting numbers on the women's arms, like tattoos or the branding of cattle, to see who would be up next.

My husband shocked me by saying, "Aren't you going to join your friends?" I thought to myself, these are not my friends. Then the women—Patty and her friends—were trying to coach me to join them. I felt peer pressure, like when I was a teenager. There is no one going to pressure me as an adult! People were going wild!

Something felt very inappropriate here. I was disgusted and could not believe or even comprehend that my husband would want to show my body off to strangers. Now, I am a nice-looking woman; I look like Lynda Carter. Not too shabby, I am thinking; but I am a good woman. I love God. God would not like this type of behavior. I was also thinking, what if my pastor could see me now? What if the mayor from my town could see me now? What if my children could see me now? I was looking into my soul and seeing my character, my whole being of "who am I?" This was not me.

I would keep my clothes on and go for a walk; maybe it would all be over with when I got back. I turned around and went on the bus to get my purse. What a sight there was on the bus: bras and shirts all over the seats. Clothing spewed everywhere; there was dead silence on the bus. But lots of noise, people drunk and out of control all around the outside of the bus. I felt so alone.

The bus driver was sitting in his seat; he was sober. I began to talk with him. I told him I could not believe what was happening. He said, "This just gets worse every year." He does not believe his company will do this another year. I told him I was going for a walk to the ladies' bathroom.

As I stepped off the bus, there were men taking water from our coolers and putting it in giant high-pressure squirt guns. I said, "What are you guys doing?" The men said, "We need water for our squirt guns for the wet T-shirt contest." I thought how perverted these men were and wondered how these women of my community could lower themselves to this level.

As I came around the corner, I had to make my way through the crowd; I saw my husband standing on a cooler that was dragged over to get a better view. He was standing there with Bill. They both looked like sick pig-men. Their mouths were wide open. He did not even care where I was or how I felt. I felt like a nothing. I did not matter. I was so upset.

Patty stopped me and asked me, "Where are you going?" I said, "Anywhere but here." She said she was sorry.

I replied, "Sorry for what?" This is not about your behavior and your choices of what you are doing. To each his own! It is my husband's sick behavior I cannot understand." I thought to myself, "Mr. Porno Man." And how many other perverts were here? This type of function can be a disguise for men to be able to gawk, grope, and partake in taking advantage of drunken women. This scene was Sodom and Gomorrah. Thanks, but no thanks! I just turned to go. I am sure everyone there could see I was so distraught. But, there he was up on the cooler!

I walked over to the restrooms; outside johns were the room of choice. The crowd was maybe two hundred people or more around the bus. I could not believe it; I was sober and amazed at what I was witnessing. I walked over to the cars and van area that was horizontal with the bus parking lot. It seemed normal over here. I watched the circus around the party bus with a nice couple I met from Cape Cod. They had a sail attached to their truck, a Buffett thing. I was not feeling too well at this point; I was not happy. But the people in that area were kicking back and enjoying the moment and that was just what I wanted to do all day. But it was far different in the bus area. The couple asked me what was going on over there and I told them. I think they felt bad for me; I was so alone. And they sure understood my concerns. They were even appalled by the actions of my husband.

We were watching when the police came to break up the crowd. I prayed it would be over by the time I went back there. I hoped my husband and his compadres would have come to their senses by then. To have the police come now, you know that is a good-sized crowd. I waited a while and then decided to go back. I thanked the couple for their company and hoped they enjoyed the show.

The crowd had thinned out; as I walked over to the bus what I witnessed sent me into shock. My husband was in line for a boob shot with his buddy Bill. The woman had no shirt on and she was very, very large-breasted.

She was easily a size 3X, and she was filling her long shot

glass up with booze for men to drink right between her breasts. I then saw a woman start squirting whipped cream on her boobs for people to lick off. She stood there, plain as day, with her chest fluffed out and her nipples waiting for more whipped cream. Both men and women were licking it off. I looked at my husband. He was into everything going on, his mouth was open like a baby looking for food, his eyes were wide open. My brain was not computing what I was seeing; it was like a big orgy. I was shocked! Men were taking their pants off, flashing themselves. I had to get out of there! I saw a man from my bus coming at me, with lots of beads around his neck. He had so many on; I would say they were at least four inches thick. The meaning was to give beads to women for a peep at their breasts. He wanted me, he was coming at me. I ran. Where was my husband: preoccupied! Husbands are supposed to keep their wives safe! I was not safe.

This whole day has been out of control. I am sober and these people are drunk. I turned to run back in the bus to get my other bag; I was scared. As I ran in between the buses, people were groping each other like in a sleazy movie. It was a scene out of a dark horror movie, where the vampires had come to drink everyone's blood. Everyone was all over each other. I got on the bus and I was crying, I was terrified and alone.

I wrote a note stating I was leaving and not to worry. I gave the note to the bus driver, so if they did a head count I was gone by my own accord. He said he felt bad that this whole event was so very ill. As I gave him my note, my husband looked right at me and then looked away. That did me in; I ran as fast as I could. I was crying so hard I could barely see where I was going. Running in between the buses was like a maze; it was endless. But when I got to the end, people were normal. I ran to the front gates and fell on the grass shaking, crying, cold, and very frightened beyond anything I could ever remember.

I was in shock, I was literally in shock! I got my cell phone out to call a friend to come and get me, but who could I call? Someone from my church? Would someone come? Who? Another mom I knew? I was shaking so hard I could barely hold onto my phone. I had only two bars of battery left! I called my friend Denise; she might come! Will she be home? Will she be busy? "Oh, my God", I cried, "Help me!"

I dialed her number. She was getting supper ready, but she said she would come get me. She knew I was upset; I was so frantic. "Please come now!" I begged. The drive was at least fifty minutes. I waited outside the gates. It was dark now. I was very cold and my whole body was trembling.

Denise came and comforted me. I have known her many years—our daughters went to preschool together, and now they are in high school. We also attended the same church; we had a great connection, especially since we had girls the same age. As we drove, I told her what had happened. We went to the Outback Steakhouse on the way home. I had my glass of wine with a good dinner, since I had not eaten and had missed the concert. I was on the grounds at the concert maybe three hours. I felt warm and safe as Denise and I sat and talked quite awhile; she is a good friend. No decent woman would have stayed in that environment, we both agreed.

She said something to me that rocked me. She said, "I do not like the way Eddie looks at me; it is as if he checks me out all over. His eyes give me the creeps." She said, "When I was a young girl, older men in the family abused me and

I know that look." She knows what it feels like to be looked at like an object. It is a look of lust, forbidden lust, and unwanted lust. "I see that in Eddie's eyes," she said. I appreciated her honesty; deep inside I knew something was distorted.

Was there something really wrong? What was I not seeing? I am trying to put it together! My brain went on overload; my body went into shock. I wanted to throw up, my stomach hurt so badly! It hurt the same way it did when he was pulling into the driveway when he came home from work at night. I was numb. I could not feel my body, but yet I was so cold. I was afraid.

Something was not right with my marriage. I saw a sick man, a man who did not love, honor, or cherish me. A man who would not lay his life down for his wife! A man who never cared what I thought or what I felt. WHY? Why was I a nothing? WHY? Why did I stay in this marriage? My vows? My children? It was Fear. It was Fear.

CHAPTER 2
REFLECTIONS

I arrived home and was greeted by the children. "Why are you home, Mom? Where's Dad?" Questions, questions! I did not want to answer any questions. But I said, "Dad is still there at the concert."

I was in a fog. I walked up the stairs; I wanted to take a shower and feel warm. I could not stop crying. I do not remember anything else except climbing into my bed and needing lots of blankets. I remember asking the children for more blankets; I was so cold.

As I lay there, I began to think about when I first met Eddie. I remember I felt a sense of distrust within myself; something was not right about him then. At that moment I brushed that feeling away and buried it inside. He was charming, as Eddie Haskell was to Mrs. Cleaver: please and thank you, let me open the door. He had the looks of John Travolta—dark blackish hair, eyes a beautiful blue. When you looked into his eyes, there was something eerie about them. There was sadness of sorts, a pitiful glaze, and a stare that could look right through to your soul. Maybe it was his eyes I should have listened to.

He pursued me like a wild tiger, relentless to its prey. Subtly, smoothly, slyly, romancing the chance to call the prey its own. Eddie would show up at my workplace, and my coworkers would tease me, "Amy, your admirer is here!" He called me constantly, talking for hours at a time. I had never had a man pursue me this way. I really thought to myself, if a guy like this could treat me this good he must love me. My minister at the time said, "He's wonderful!" My friends, my family, and even myself. I called him just that—Mr. Wonderful. He told my family he had never been happier in his whole life.

Eddie was attentive to my two-year-old Danny; he even purchased a big-wheel motorized truck for the little guy. Anytime we went somewhere, he carried Danny on his shoulders when his little feet could not keep up. We were all he ever needed. I thought he was all Danny and I ever needed. But there were things I did not see, nor did I want to see. The writing was on the wall; it should have slapped me right upside the head and woken me up. Sort of like a bad dream when you just start to drift off to sleep and a big jolt flows through your body. Yet it did not wake me.

Mr. Wonderful married me on July 17th, 1988. One week before the wedding, I felt something was not right with this guy. I went to his Mom and talked to her about my feelings. He was busy—too busy for Danny and me. He would leave early, come home late; he was always with and helping his friends. Something changed: was it my imagination or maybe was I being needy? I felt ignored, cast aside! Here I was, a beautiful woman, business background, smart; I had it all going for me. I wanted to be a mom and a wife as did any woman who grew up with a Cinderella syndrome. His mom told me, "He has taken on a family, and that is a big responsibility. Give him time." Time never changed a thing. I cried and I cried.

I was then pregnant with his child and felt completely alone. As my body grew with a child, he moved emotionally further away. I told him my feelings of loneliness; I married to have a best friend and soul mate, not a stranger. I wanted my husband to have a heart and be a husband and father. Instead, he called me, "A big, fat pig." He told me he "hated my belly!" I could not believe what he said! Sexually we had nothing and emotionally we had nothing. I was beside myself! I found a good counselor and went crying uncontrollably, with Danny in tow. That did not help. The doctor told me I was just pregnant and over-emotional. He said, "Leave him or make the best of it." I was now a mom, not a woman, to Eddie. I did not deserve this treatment. What was wrong with me? He was not even attracted to me. But I am beautiful!

Within the first year, he would walk right by us when he came home. I remember driving to a Billy Joel concert—the first big outing after our daughter, Emily, was born. He never spoke to me on that drive. I looked out the window from Worcester to Hartford and cried—silently—so he would not hear me nor see my tears. I was lonely. That night, at the show, he laughed and talked to my brother who met us there. He interrupted me whenever I spoke. I wondered, "Was I an alien?" Mr. Wonderful did not exist. Never did. I married the wrong man.

I feel alone right now as I lay in this bed. My brain is on overdrive. I would question him why he treated me the way he did. Always ignoring me, never caring for my feelings, or concerns, I wanted a husband, a mate, but the response was always scary. He would snap and say to me, "It's all in your head! Quit complaining!" I realized that he was a bully. I really felt crazy. Maybe it WAS me? I questioned my sanity with him daily. As time went on, I could see there were issues, some type of attention deficient problem and obsessive/compulsive behavior. He seemed to use anger to mask the uproars.

As years passed, I stayed for my children, marriage vows, and the commitment of the Bible's words I honored. I thought maybe another child would change him. I was blessed with twin boys after Emily: Kevin and Kyle. But it never changed Eddie's heart. He could not pay attention. He ignored us all. I learned not to disturb the lion because his roar was loud very loud.

I remember a day when he was on his recliner watching TV, and Emily came running into the room crying about something that had happened outside. She ran right to his chair, crying. She was proceeding to tell him what happened, and he screamed at her, "SHUT UP!" His mouth was open wide. He was annoyed that she was disturbing him. She started to whimper and catch her breath, like a person who is asthmatic, who cannot breathe! She was so upset and was trying to talk, but she was shaking. Then he said, "Stop your sniveling! Toughen up!" A ton of bricks hit me right upside the head. She was me. She was me!

That little girl of maybe six years old was me. She was treated like a nothing, she did not matter. She was a beautiful child; she loved her little ponies, her Barbie's, her toys, and her life. She sang always to her little brothers all the nursery rhymes, such as, "I'm a little Tea Pot," and also the song "Achey Breaky Heart." She would run through the big Victorian home we lived in, squealing with sounds of joy, singing, and dancing. I was a stay-at-home mom. I loved it and I loved being a mom; it filled all my needs.

On this day I saw something ugly; I knew ugly, I was living it. I cried for my lovely daughter. I told him, "The way she was just treated will ruin her life and her outlook on men. There was no need of that. Can't you just stop and talk to her? Can't you hear her heart? It might be something simple to us, but to her it was big and it hurts." I was talking to him about her but it was also about me. I was mad! I was angry! I was sad! I wanted to leave! I didn't even wait for a response. I went to tend to my emotionally wounded daughter. As a result of my standing up for my girl, he did get a little better with her after that. Soon after, I took my wedding rings off; I heard them clink with a loud echo on the glass table top. "I will not wear them again until you act like a husband to me," I told him.

Being with him was like a ticking time bomb. Tick, Tick, is it a good day? Or will it be a bad day? I compare it to a puzzle; it looks good when it is all together. Then when it comes apart, if you do it enough times, the cardboard paper gets thin and unraveled. Then it is hard to keep putting the pieces together. Then it does not look as good. Perfect home, perfect careers, perfect children; it all looks so good. For him, it was knowing the right councilman, the right policeman, the right state representative, the right neighbor, the right business owner, the right men. He looked good to all his male friends. A trophy wife that was perfection at its finest.

All of these thoughts were running through my head as

I lay there after the concert, waiting to see if he was even coming home and what condition he might be in. I wanted him to change! But somehow I knew, deep down in my soul, he was never going to change, never.

Our marriage had always been rocky. He could not love me the way I needed him to; the way I thought any woman needed to be loved. He was ALWAYS angry, his face was angry. He did not want to be bothered by his family, but it all looked so good to family and neighbors. I was dying inside. The memories of my life with him were swimming around my brain. My brain was trying to compute, shuffle, and make sense of what just happened today. He did cross a line today at the concert—a big line!

My mind drifted to a time when I was invited to my neighbor's house across the street for their son's birthday. The twins were about two years old. We went as a family. It was far from a family day. He got a beer and ignored me and the twins; he just huddled with the other men there. He loved being in the company of men, or those whom he thought were men.

Any idea what it is like watching two-year-old twin boys? They were everywhere! And I was responsible for their lives! Something different was happening to me that I did not understand, something within my soul. My coping instincts were changing; I panicked over watching the boys. I realized at this moment that the responsibility was solely mine. I had to learn how to cope without my husband. Had I gone over and asked for help, he would have made me feel like an idiot. They were too active for me to handle alone. I remember thinking, "I cannot do this!" I lunged forward and put my arms around both of the boys, picked them up and left. I told my friend and neighbor I had to go home. I left, watching him drink, laugh, and enjoy himself. When he realized I had left he came and found me. The boys were playing in the dining room and I was in the kitchen.

The beast was home. "What the fuck is your problem?"— he roared and screamed, and then I saw the tiger. The foul language and thoughts that were streaming out of his mouth made no sense. Then a chair was thrown at me; it hit the island in the kitchen. He could not hear my pleas to listen to my heart and understand. I was scared, incredibly scared.

But it was my poor daughter who was frightened; she saw and heard it all and ran for help. Emily went across the street to my best friend Kay's house. At the very moment Kay came over, he walked out and drove away. I cried. My daughter cried. I wanted him to change. I called his mom, crying. I told her what happened she said, "Let him rant and rave, when he is like that. He will calm down and get over it. He did that when he was young and I would let him have his temper tantrums and then he would be okay." This behavior was promoted!!

Just like today, at this moment, I think to myself, "Oh, my God, what is going to happen when he gets home?" I am starting to feel frightened at the thought of him coming home from the concert. I need to stay on alert and be vigilant tonight. Maybe he will come in and pass out; that would be better than any of my other thoughts.

He is a fireman, a national guardsman, a serviceman. The fact that he liked being with men was comforting in a sense because, I thought, it was better than being with other women. I had questioned if he was gay or bisexual. I had noticed that if certain men did not interest him he would ignore them. Men that drank beer, talked nasty, and were nice-looking; he could belly up and be friends with. But men who were short, or small, or the kind of men that were dainty in any way, he could not bond with. His friends seemed not to have good relationships with their own wives. They talked badly about them to others, just as I believe he did about me.

Oh, but I had no idea about everything that he did or was doing. Being a fireman, we had scanners and beepers under pillows, on headboards, in the kitchen, in the bathrooms, and in the cars. They would shock me into life, especially in the middle of the night. Or frighten my nerves, like in a horror movie when the creature would seem to jump out of the screen. Or when Freddie from *Nightmare on Elm Street* would just slit a throat or be waiting behind a shower curtain with an axe for his next victim. I was on the edge, always on edge.

He came in and out of the bedroom all hours of the night, slamming doors. The worst thing was his heavy feet. He stomped his feet when he walked; it would go right through me, like the sound of an earthquake rumbling and trembling. I waited for the aftershocks. I stayed quiet. The children knew and experienced the same sounds and tantrums from him. I worked two nights a week at BOSE Corporation and the boys knew the wrath of the father. They tested him every night as children do.

There came a time when he needed to get his certificate stating he was a "real" fireman. He had never gone to the firefighting academy; he did not ever want to go. He always blamed me and our marriage, lack of money, or his second job. He just did not want to deal with it. He eventually did go for one day and then he came home. The fire department put him in lockdown for counseling, to try to help him. He did do well for a while, he was calmer. At the onsite rehab, he admitted he was an alcoholic and had anger issues; he told me this when he got home. I thought maybe we had a chance to get it together. Little did I know "Eddie Haskell" was working his charms. I found out later he was talking to a woman police officer from New Jersey from the lockdown at home. He was hoping to go see her on his way home from Florida. Unbelievable!

I know that, as I am waiting for him to come home, I am shaking, crying, and cold, and unable to comprehend what I witnessed at this concert. But what I saw was so much more than crude behavior by upstanding citizens of the community. I saw a sick man, my husband. I saw sickness; I saw glimpses of my life with him today. This day has changed my life; it rocked my world, and I the saw truth, the ugly, messy truth.

I had caught him a few times watching pornography. Like the time I went downstairs in the morning when it was snowing; I wanted to watch the news to see if the children had school. He looked at me and said, "I fell asleep watching the weather again." I turned on the 42-inch TV to find a very large sex scene happening with sound. I said, "Nice. Thank God one of the children did not come down here first." On the day of this event it all came together, all the years of deceit. I thought he loved himself better than he loved me. He could just turn women off with a remote! He had absolutely no respect for women. I knew my marriage was over that day. He needed help; help that I could not give him.

My heart felt like it was broken and was ripped out of my chest. I cried out to God, "Please help me! I feel dead!" I needed help and there was no one there to help me.

CHAPTER 3
THE DEPARTURE

Bang! I woke to the slamming door. He was home. My heart started racing almost out of control. I lay there in the dark, I lay still and quiet. I was afraid. I looked at the clock; it was three-thirty. I heard the heavy foot thumps coming up the stairs.

Eddie came into the bedroom, took his clothes off, got into our bed and said, "What the fuck is your problem? It was just a little wet T-shirt contest!"

I said to him, "It was way more than that!" I really did not want to say too much at three-thirty in the morning. He reeked of alcohol.

To my surprise, he started telling me about what happened at the concert. I guess Bill got so drunk he ended up at the emergency medical treatment area. He was throwing up very badly. His wife was crying; she thought he was going to end up in the hospital dying of alcohol poisoning. Bill spent most of his time there and missed the concert.

Eddie said, "My friends felt bad for me that you left." He said he stayed on the bus by himself and did not even see the concert. Now, it was all my fault! Something unusual was happening; he was not yelling or being angry. I was thinking that something happened there that I did not know about. I could only imagine. But he started snoring and was out like a light.

Well, morning came and I got up out of bed quietly and went to the kitchen. I sat down at the kitchen table, looked over at the door, and I felt an extraordinary presence with me. My body shook and I felt such tears wanting to pour out; what a sad awakening. I heard a voice inside my soul say, "He has to go." It was unbelievable to hear those four words. I had to trust this voice! It was a supernatural presence. I listened and I knew with no uncertainty that my husband had to go. I trusted the voice I heard. I felt so numb! It was all so clear; I could not go on this way anymore. We always brushed things under the rug. He would not listen to anything I ever had to say. He would yell, "You always have to be right! You are not my mother!" He twisted things and the conversations we would have and made me feel crazy. I was always overreacting—so he said.

Now I am sitting here thinking that I know I am sane and I am hurt. If he loves the children he will go get help. We need to separate, even just for a while. Just to see things clearly for once would be such a blessing. He has to go so he can see what he has done. Crazy-making!! I needed the peace so badly! He cannot just go out drinking, come home and pass out, and go on living like nothing happened. He did this when he was a "weekend warrior" as I call it; he was in the National Guard for a while. He would get so drunk with his comrades, come home late, yell at the children, and then pass out on the couch. He smelled of an all- nighter. We knew to get out of his way on those Sunday nights. I also caught him watching pornography back then a few times in the middle of the night at our old home. Everything was making sense. My brain is trying to put it all together. It is too much to handle, and all I know is something horrible happened to me yesterday. I am not the same person; I am in such a fog. God help me! I prayed and I cried. He has to go. The voice said so! No, I am not insane! This might be the first sane thing I will ever do for myself. I am afraid.

Can I let him go? Can I do this to the children? Can he change? He cannot love me, not like this! I knew deep in my soul, I knew with my whole being, he had to go. I had no doubt in my mind. I needed to be obedient to my inner spirit. What was in store for my future? It was as if a feeling of imminent death was upon me. My life was built around him and my children; now I was going to end it. I knew that life as we knew it would never be the same, after today. Death was an impending feeling.

I remember the day my brother Phil died when I was fifteen. I felt death that day. I feel it now. It is an unbelievable feeling of disbelief, a tragic memory that never goes away.

My mind drifted back to that day. I was home and I awoke too early for a teenager. I could not go back to sleep. "But I need to sleep," I thought. My dog, Pepper, was whining to go out, so I got up to let her out. I was home alone with my step-mom, Lisa, and Pepper. My Dad and brothers had gone on a camping weekend, just the boys. Pepper was crying to come back in; I thought that was too quick because she stays out longer than that. I was fully awake by now, so I turned on the television and was watching a movie about a cruise ship sinking; people were scared and drowning. Then the phone rang, and I almost came out of my skin. I got up to answer it. Lisa was still sleeping. It was my Dad. He was screaming, "Phil is gone! Phil is gone, you have to come now."

"Dad, where are you?" I said. He began to describe where he was, and I realized I knew that area well. As a teenager that was my turf, the Verde River. My friends and I would all go white-water tubing on weekends, but today was not going to be a picnic. My Dad had never sounded like this; he could not find my brother. I woke up Lisa, and yelled for her to pick up the phone. She told Dad we were on our way. I remember getting in the car, but the trip there was a blur.

I remember Lisa saying, "Phil is hiding, he must be hiding in the woods." As I pulled into the camping area, I saw my Dad. He was hitting his head up against a tree—what a horrible sight that was. We jumped out of the car; he was making no sense at all. He was crying about Phil being gone and while my other brother, Dean, was being rescued. The ambulance was there and they had just brought Dean toward the ambulance. Dean and Phil had gone swimming. Phil was not a strong swimmer, and the undercurrent caught them. They went under.

Dean kept screaming, "I could not hold on to him! I could not hold on to him!" The EMTs took my Dad and Dean to the hospital; they told us to follow them. The rescue people said they would call when they found him. I drove to the hospital; I remember being in a fog. This was not happening! When we arrived at the hospital my dad's best friend, Charlie, was there. I volunteered to go back with him and drive my dad's truck back and get all the camping gear. I needed to feel useful in some way. Was I drawn to go? Maybe. I was a caregiver—I always took care of my brothers and my dad; that was the codependent part of my personality that I displayed.

As Charlie and I pulled up, I lost it! I saw my brother Phil's feet hanging out of a body bag. I saw his shoes, the shoes he wore; he was only thirteen years old. He had not lived yet! Why? It hit me that hard—he was gone, not lost, but dead. The rescue team came to the car and asked me, the only relative there, to identify my brother. I looked at Charlie; he must have seen the pain on my face as I said, "Charlie can you do it? I can't." I was a happy junior in high school; my life was ahead of me. But I felt like imminent death was upon me. What was in store for my family's future?

Our lives changed after that day. We had a memorial for my brother in Arizona; lots of people came. My Dad was senior master sergeant in the air force, serving in the Korean and Vietnam Wars. I swear, the whole base showed up! My Dad was a well-respected man. The family then flew to Washington, D.C., and we had another memorial, a funeral, and a military burial at Arlington National Cemetery, where my father will be laid to rest with Phil one day. Back then they flew planes overhead after the traditional twenty-one-gun salute. To this day, I get tears in my eyes when I see that formation of planes flying overhead. I am proud to have come from a military family. I am proud of my Dad and his service to our country. My heart aches for military families, the trauma of war, the addictions, yet I feel proud.

Today, as I sit at this kitchen table, I have the same feeling of death. The same feeling of disbelief; the unbelievable act and actions of my husband has turned on some light in my soul. As I thought about death being a permanent ending, I wondered if there was any hope. There was no hope when they found my brother.

There was a time I had hoped my grandpa would wake up and not die. He had a heart attack at home only two months before Eddie and I were married. The hospital had Grandpa on life support until my dad could fly in from Honduras, where his rank was equivalent to a colonel, training the Honduran Air Force the egress part of maintenance on airplanes. My dad was the eighth-top person in the United States to do this. He had done the same thing in Saudi Arabia after Phil died.

When my dad arrived at the hospital, the doctors removed my grandpa from life support, but Grandpa kept breathing. My cousins and aunt came to the hospital; we talked and prayed loudly so Grandpa could hear us. We rubbed his legs and said, "Grandpa, wake up." We all had so much hope.

We all loved him so much; he had a big passion for baseball. My grandpa played for the Boston Braves in the National League for a short time, and he was good at baseball. But he could not play the sport as a career due to financial reasons: he had to support the family and there was no money in baseball back then. Grandpa ended up playing in his later years for the old-timers' games. He was a good old gentleman and loved his grandkids.

Grandpa always had a garden; we would always help him pick whatever vegetable or fruit was in season. He had the best strawberries I have ever had. My dad would tell us such stories of growing up during Prohibition. He told us that Grandpa brewed beer in Grandma's washer one time; he bottled it and planted the beer in the garden to age. The law officers never found it there. Grandpa even built us a camp house in the backyard, so when we visited his house we could be loud, listen to ball games, sing and dance, read *National Geographic* magazines and of course *Mad* magazine, and comic books also. It was our space with Grandpa.

Now I could only hope he would wake up. But he did not. I loved him so much. My grandpa fell asleep forever, and hope died. I remember Grandpa's funeral. Eddie did not even sit with me; he sat with his own mother. I sat at the back of the chapel and saw Eddie laughing and being with his mom. It made me sad that he would not even comfort me; I thought it was as if he was there because of the social gathering. That was a red flag I should have seen, a big red flag. But I was burying my grandfather! I could not deal with Eddie right then. I was so distraught, I felt alone and numb, seeing Eddie behave this way. But my brothers, cousins, aunts, uncles, and Dad—we were all just so devastated; we grieved together. I just brushed my feelings away with Eddie's actions; he did apologize later for being insensitive only after I had to tell him how rude he was to me. He basically ignored me and was very attentive to his mother.

   In death, my brother was gone, and so was the hope I had for my grandfather to wake up, I wondered, was there hope Eddie would wake up and be kind, respectful, and loving? I, Amy wanted that hope, God wanted that hope, but my inner spirit knew beyond anything that I could rationalize that there was no hope. I needed to prepare for the worst. In death you prepare; but nothing could prepare me for the death I faced here on earth. I was frightened about what was in store from Eddie's wrath. I wanted hope so badly!

   What is about to start will become a big blur; I am

overwhelmed. Eddie is awake; I can hear him stomping around. When he walks he stomps loudly, his walk is so heavy, as in the movies of *Jack and the Beanstalk*, when the giant would say, "fee fi fo fum"; boom, boom, and the giant would be coming to find you. Eddie gave me the feeling that he was going to find me and smooth things over, or I was going to get the brunt of his fury. He is coming down the stairs now and I feel like I am in shock; who am I?

He saw me sitting there at the kitchen table; everything just came out of me. "You have to go, Eddie, I cannot live this way, you have to go!" I can only remember him saying, "No problem, I will find a place as soon as possible."

I cannot breathe, I do not know what happened, but he is leaving. I had hoped things could change, but he is very willing to go.

Eddie did find a place to rent for just a few months, he told me. The apartment he was renting was going to be torn down to make way for a parking lot. And how convenient— the apartment was near the fire station; he would surely feel at home now.

I thought, maybe he will change and come home. I was confused with unwarranted hope. It all happened so fast; the next thing I knew he had a few of the firemen come to help him move. It was awful. I wanted none of the men from the concert coming into my home, I told Eddie. I was so disgusted with all that, but I am looking at his behavior and how disgusted I am, and was, with him. In my opinion, he needed help for porn addiction, and help with the way he treats me and the children. I saw a bully and an emotional abuser when I looked at him. He has to be willing to look at what it has done to our family. He cannot hear me! He is deaf! Here were all these men in our home moving Eddie out; my husband, my children's father, it was just not real.

I was crying when one of the firemen came over to me and asked if I was okay. Tom is a good guy. He had no idea what had happened. Or at least any truth about what went on behind the four walls of our home. I said, "I do not know, but thank you for asking." Someone cared. It was all so sad.

I gave Eddie our bedroom set and extra beds so the children would have somewhere to sleep when they went to his apartment. I went over- board and bought him dishes and silverware, and gave him bedding, pillows, everything to make it easy on him and the kids—until we could decide what was going on.

I went upstairs, when the men were done up there, and sat in our office where we had a business setup. I did not know where to start. I sat in front of the computer and had no idea even how much money we had or where to begin looking. I began to cry, and Eddie walked in and looked at me and said, "You are pathetic. By the time I am done with you, you will have no house, no car, no kids, no nothing!" I felt like I was just slapped upside the head. This man did not care about me—he never had; he would brag about how much he loved me to our families and friends, but no one ever saw how it really was. I am not crazy! That comment was a shocker; I saw the cruelty in his eyes. This was the beginning of his revenge. He was telling people I threw him out of the house! I had asked him to leave to get help. Now I only felt threatened.

This is the beginning of hell on earth and Eddie's deceit.

CHAPTER 4
A FOG

That was it. He was gone. Moved out of our beautiful three-story Victorian home. I collapsed onto my bed and cried. The cries that came from my body, my lungs, my throat, my inner core sounded like the death of all deaths. Like an animal that was caught in a trap, not a box trap, but a claw trap. The kind of claw trap that brings blood and death. I had never cried like that in my life. My head hurt so badly and my eyes were bloodshot and swollen. What was I going to do now? I was thinking of my lack of finances and of being alone. He said I would have nothing by the time he was done with me! I knew him! I was afraid and hurt at the same time!

I had been on a FMLA, or Family Medical Leave, from BOSE Corporation. Just before the concert I was diagnosed with having Post Traumatic Stress Disorder, or PTSD, due to an automobile accident a few years before. The combination of having trouble with my marriage, the PTSD, and the stress of it all was absolutely getting to me. Between Eddie, work, and taking care of the children, it just was too much. I also missed having Kay, my dear friend, as my neighbor. Her husband had taken a job out of state and they had moved. We had raised our kids together, and now I really felt alone.

Eddie never helped out much at home; heck, he was never home. When he was home he was unavailable. I was just like a single mom but at least I had financial backing. I had been a stay-at-home mom for ten years and did sales for home parties. I loved being home with my children, but I felt like a trapped animal. It was like pulling teeth to get Eddie to relieve me of any household duties.

I remember going food shopping with the twins; I would pile the food on them and all around them in the double stroller. I could not take them shopping and push a cart all by myself. And if I did get a chance to go alone, Eddie made me feel like I had to hurry home or he might hurt one of them; it was an uncomfortable feeling. He would do this manipulation thing on me so I would feel compelled to hurry back. I was not peaceful when I went anywhere, and I had to hurry back. He did this one day in front of his mom; I looked at her and said, "Look at what he just did! We need to get back quickly!" Even she said, "That is not right!" And she told him so; he got better after his mom said something to him. But that did not undo the damage he was doing to me! I felt like a trapped animal!

When the twins were about three, I could take no more—I needed to get away. I went to see my brother, Timmy, in Florida, my first vacation alone in ten years. I had peace and quiet there; I remember going to the airport to head home, and Timmy dropped me off. He gave me a hug good-bye, and I broke down and cried.

Timmy said, "Hey, Sis, I will be up in a few months. It is okay!" He thought I was crying because I was going to miss him. It really was because I did not want to go home! I think Eddie's whole family thought I was a primadonna to go on a vacation alone. They had no idea what my life was like, none! They never really liked me; I felt I was never good enough for the baby of the family. He was his Mommy's Tiger. The whole family put him on a pedestal, I kid you not, and he even told me they put him on a pedestal. So here is this perfect father, fireman, husband, and breadwinner, and his wife complains and lashes out! I wonder why!

I was in business before I had stayed home with my children, so when they got to school age I decided to find a good job. I found one, and my escape was work! I applied for the position at BOSE Corporation and got it! I loved working for BOSE; I was the unsung hero one year, and I was a top achiever. I was happy, until it all started to unravel!

The accident was just a catalyst, a slow burn compared to what was really happening inside of me.

I remember the day of the accident like it was yesterday. My friend, Faith, and I had gone to the Christmas Tree Shoppe. We loved shopping there! We were on our way home, and I drove the back way home on Route 240. It was a gorgeous ride through that part of New England, and it was on this day when it happened: I was driving, when all of a sudden I saw a large boulder come rolling down the side of the hill to my right. I thought this must be a freak thing, an act of Mother Nature! I screamed to my friend Faith "Hang On!" There was no way to avoid the boulder and I knew all too well about car accidents.

I had tangled with a semi-truck years before in a small sports car. I lived through that! But in that instance with the boulder, I felt like I was back in that sports car hanging on for dear life. My body jolted back and forth, I heard the sounds of grinding metal and I remembered being in my sports car and passing out from shock. It was such a shock, seeing the nose of my car heading underneath the trucker's rig, I blacked out! I felt the same on the impact of the boulder; it all happened so fast. It was like a flash—a feeling of familiarity at that instant of a moment—deja vu!

This boulder was big! Route 240 was a two-lane road and I had nowhere to go. I held on to the steering wheel for dear life; I held on and steered the van straight. I thought I was going to die! I knew if I swerved I would roll my van. I heard the horrible screeching of metal and loud bangs like the sound of guns. I felt the van shake, with lots of noise; it happened so fast! The next thing I knew I was pulling the van over with all the strength I had, into sand on the road's edge.

"Oh, my God!" I thought—I am still alive! I looked at Faith and said, "Are you okay?"

"Yes," she said.

We got out of the van to check the damage; both of my tires were blown out on the right side of the vehicle. I looked underneath the van and saw that the boulder had run all the way underneath. The undercarriage was badly damaged and the two tires were popped. But oh, I had the most horrible headache! I told Faith I was going to go use the phone at one of the homes across the street to call Eddie and the police.

I walked over to a beautiful red rustic home and knocked on the door. A nice elderly man answered the door right away. I said, "May I use your phone to call the police and my husband? I have been in an accident."

The man was so kind. "Why yes, of course," he said. I called the police and explained where my van was, and then I called Eddie to come. I was only fifteen minutes from home

He said, "I will be right there."

At about the time I hung up, there was a knock on the door. It was a middle-aged man who lived up the street. Both men knew each other.

The man from up the street looked at me and said, "I saw who did this to you!"

I asked myself, what is he talking about? I said, "A boulder came out of nowhere; that's all."

He said, "No, ma'am, I saw boys rolling rocks down the hill earlier and then I saw them push the big one down the hill as your van came up the road!" He said, "You are lucky you were not killed!"

Wow! I could not believe someone would do something like this on purpose! I was absolutely stunned! I felt numb! My head hurt and I had the biggest headache ever. I thought I must be really stressed to have a whopper of a headache like this.

I looked at the man and said, "Will you talk to the police and tell them what you told me?" He agreed and said he would do whatever I needed. He was almost angry that these kids did this to me. I thanked them both for everything and went back to my van. I told Faith what the men had said. Like me, Faith could not believe someone would do that.

Then we could hear children; the sound was coming from the top of the hill. Were they looking to see if we were okay? Were they looking to see how much damage was done? But we could hear them laughing and talking…

The police officer pulled up in front of my van. Faith and I explained what happened; I just remember I kept telling the officer I had a horrible headache. The officer went to the house at the top of the hill and talked to the boys—there were three of them. When the officer came back to the scene he said, "The boys admitted they did it; the father of one of the boys tried to make it look like it was not their fault. But yes, they did it." The officer said he was going to speak to the witness and file his report. The officer said he could not believe I did not roll the van, or that no one was coming from the opposite direction. I was so very lucky.

Eddie came to the scene to assess the damages; we needed to get the van to a shop. Eddie said he would take care of it. He seemed to be put out by the whole thing. It interrupted his day—he had been mowing the lawn, Kay told me so later. He drove Faith and me back to our house, and I complained about my headache; I felt out of sorts. I remember going into the house and getting a glass of water from the water cooler. As I dispensed the water, the glass slipped out of my hands. I could not feel it; I had a hold of it, but I just felt so numb. The glass fell and shattered all over the floor. My cousin, Leanne, and Faith saw what happened. My head hurt and I just needed to sit. I felt weak and dizzy.

I went and sat down on the couch; I felt very weird. I remember Leanne sitting with me on the couch for a while; I just wanted quiet. It was so comforting to know she had always been there for me, even if it was just to sit quietly. I waited till the next day to go to the doctor.

In my opinion, looking back, don't you think a fireman should have taken his wife to the hospital? I drove myself to my doctor's office the next day. I was diagnosed with a concussion and whiplash. My neck and head hurt so badly! I have been out of sorts since the accident. I had a numb feeling and I could not think clearly. It had to have been the jolt I took when the boulder hit the vehicle.

The doctor prescribed rest and much physical therapy and Motrin. I had a home and four children to take care of, and I was hurt! Talk about needing help! I could barely function! Thus began therapy for my body and my mind.

I had been going to counseling all along because our marriage had been on the rocks almost since the day we were married. Eddie even came to see the same counselor, but Eddie could not manage to keep his appointments. Eventually I went alone. After the auto accident, things between us got worse. I remember coming home and telling Eddie what the counselor had said: that I had Post Traumatic Stress Disorder.

Some things started to make sense—why Eddie's stomping bothered me, why his yelling and temper tantrums bothered me. He would come home all hours of the night. I think that was worst! I would be sound asleep and BANG!! He would burst into the room in the middle of the night—slamming doors and turning lights on; the house would shake when he came home. That scared the crap out of me. He was scary to me; he was the big bad wolf!

When he yelled and blocked doorways or twisted conversations he was hurting my whole being! I felt intimidated! I tried so very hard to ask for help; I got on the computer and printed out all that I could. I read up on PTSD. I was like a veteran of war. But how could that be? I remember talking to Eddie and giving him the articles I had researched on the Internet so he could help me sort it out. The articles stayed on the nightstand for one night, and then the papers were on the floor. He never once picked them up. He never once cared what was happening to me. He actually made my PTSD worse! I felt like he was psychologically unavailable and the mind control he projected on me was confusing to my very soul. Life with Eddie was confusing!

Now here I am; he is gone; I cannot function, and I am a mess.

I was not sleeping or eating appropriately. I tried to go to back to work at BOSE because Eddie was making it hard for me financially. He was withholding money from me and the children. He had always done our finances, because it was "his money." He worked hard for "his money" and he would spend it the way "he wanted to." I had to go ask my pastor and the church for help. Pastor called Eddie and had a talk with him and said, "You cannot do that to Amy and the children. That is not right!" Pastor was not happy and he told me so. Pastor Paul saw a side of Eddie that I saw and which he, Pastor, understood. But yet, his goal was to try and save a marriage according to God's word. I felt there was more that he was not saying about his conversations with Eddie at this time—I could tell. Was it based on men being men, protecting one another, maybe? Or was it the confidentiality oath a pastor takes? Or was Pastor Paul protecting me and the children—I wondered.

I was totally in shock—for my life! What a tidal wave had come through the middle of my world and my children's! I had to resign from BOSE—I just could not perform my job to my full potential. I was ON GAURD at work, I felt so much pressure, and I trusted NO ONE! At this point in time I needed a mindless job because I could not think sensibly. I had no money, so I needed to work. I could not fail! I could not fail my children. They were the most precious things in my life. I could not go back on FMLA; the money that program offered was not enough!

When Eddie left, he left totally! I was responsible for the mortgage, the taxes, all the utilities, the car payment, food for the children—everything! I was afraid! I felt like he wanted me to suffer! For what? His sins? He was hurting me but I could see he was also hurting his children! I was in panic mode to survive. He wanted me to have nothing. But oh, my God, I thought—what was his reasoning that he would also leave his children with nothing? I wondered how a man could do this!!

He was vengeful to me but yet his reaction to people was that I broke his heart. This was so confusing to me. He told people I threw him out and it was all me to blame; he told Pastor just that. Yet to me, to my face, he said he wanted me gone. His hatred showed in his actions and in his words to me. The children had witnessed his atrocious behavior to me and toward them. They knew, and I knew, why. Why could no one else see? Eddie even said to me, "Just get over it!" He expected me to just get over a fifteen-year marriage! The children could not understand. I could not understand. Nothing made sense!

Eddie and I had signed up for a marriage class at the church we had been attending before the Jimmy Buffett concert. I thought to myself, "Well, that is the answer! He will change! He will surely see the light! God will help!" But that was wishful thinking.

I called the church and met with the church secretary, Joan. We went out to breakfast and I told her what had happened at the concert. Everything! I held nothing back. It was a scene from Sodom and Gomorrah! I cried so much, telling her all that happened. I swear she is an angel friend. While we were sitting there, the youth pastor came into the restaurant looking for me, (the restaurant is near the church) and he sat down with us. He said, "Why did you have your husband leave your marital home? This is not right!" I could not tell him all that happened at the concert, all the years of emotional abuse and stress, all the years of feeling alone with Eddie, and all the years of pornography. I just looked at him and said, "He had to go! I needed peace from him so badly! Talk to Pastor Paul! He knows the details."

What happened at that concert was not how a good man acts to his wife. What happened at that concert has me in shock. I am numb, I am lost, I am hurt; I have realized my husband needs to change his ways. Eddie needed professional help but he refused to accept that fact. I felt like my life was over! I have lived through a nightmare! The youth pastor had no idea—none of what I was living through. He is a man's man type of guy, so he liked Eddie.

I did agree to come to the marriage class, if Eddie would. Again, thoughts of hope! Pastor Paul said Eddie will come.

So here we are at a marriage class with ten couples— talking about nice things husbands do for their wives and how nicely they treat each other. And Eddie pipes up and confesses how much he loves me and wants to make our marriage work, bragging about me and what a good mom and wife I am...I wanted to run, my insides shook! It took all I had inside me not to stand up in that class and scream—LIAR! LIAR!!!

If I had I would have looked like a nutcase! I wanted to say, "Oh, if you all could have just seen him at a Jimmy

Buffett concert a few weeks ago. And, oh, if you all could see and hear inside the four walls of my home!" God help me!

He is also spending his life at the bar, especially now that he has moved. The children and I see his vehicle at the local club! He told my mom, "I am going to drink more and all I want now!" And oh, I am supposed to be the alcoholic!

I called him one night, crying and hoping to talk; a woman answered the phone and laughed at me! He was at the bar, and they were laughing and making fun of me.

He said, "Why are you bothering me?" You have no idea, I wanted to tell him! How crazy is this?

I wanted out of that marriage class while he was saying those things. How could he mean all that! It was bull! I wanted no part of that class. He needed the help, not me! Yes, I have PTSD, but his issues are bigger than the boogeyman's are to me. What kind of mind games are these! I left that class so fast I did not even say good-bye to anyone. I cried all the way home. My shock just kept mounting! I cried out to God again and again! Help me! What do I do? I feel numb!! My head feels like someone shook me really hard. I felt like I was not even attached to own my body.

I did not go back to that marriage class. I could not put myself through that again! I went and told the pastor I was not coming back and why. I told him everything, and I cried and cried. I could not contain my emotions. He said that God would always be there for me, but I needed more help than he could give me. I said, "Pastor, what I need is peace in my life."

I wanted peace so badly! Peace from Eddie! Eddie needed to change. He needed to be kind! He needed to love, to honor, and to cherish me. He took those vows, too! Looking back, no one should have put me through what happened that night. The leadership there should have helped me and talked to me, but they did not know the real story. The mental confusion Eddie caused me was like a hot iron to my soul. He projected that it was me with the issues, not him!

What I do know is that I needed the safety of my church. Every Sunday I took the children to Sunday school and service. Every Sunday I sat in the back row and cried. I just needed to hear God's word; I needed to hear about what was good. I know God loves me, he knows all about me! He knows I am a good person, a good mother, he knows my integrity, my honesty, and he knows I loved my husband no matter what. God knows every hair on my head and he's known me always! I will always be his child and be loved by him. No one can take that away from me, no one!

During this time I could not get enough of God's word. I went to church on Sunday mornings, Sunday nights, women's Bible study, and ladies' night out. I sat listening quietly, not saying anything to anyone. If I did start to talk, I would cry, so I determined I would be quiet. I was a zombie, I felt like a zombie! I was in eternal shock! I had to live each moment of my life in faith or I would crumble!

No one knows how I am feeling or what I have been through. Just Joan, my angel friend—she knew about trauma. She reached out to me on many occasions, and I trusted her. I wasn't able to trust anyone else; everyone thought I was the bad one. Even a few of my own family members believed in Eddie's version of our troubles. I was an outcast; I was blackballed and called crazy and ill by him to my face. How cruel was this? Why would he do this to me? I was just trying to survive and get through and come out sane! My sanity came from within, only because of my spiritual relationship with God.

I remember one day lying on my bed, just crying so hard; I was praying and talking to God, "Help me, I feel so lost!" And again I heard that distinctive voice say, "You are not lost—you are found!"

I know beyond anything in this world that there is a God who has hold of my hand and is leading me from this hell! The road is very rough and I need to keep focused on my path!

I remember one communion Sunday, between serving the bread and the wine, Pastor Paul started singing quietly, the song "He lead—eth me, He lead—eth me! By his own hand He lead-eth me! His faith-ful

fol-l'wer I would be, For by his hand He lead-eth me."

The whole church quietly sang along with him. It was beautiful! I cried and sang quietly with him and my church family. Just a quiet moment, an intimate moment, a peaceful moment with our spiritual being.

CHAPTER 5
THE CHILDREN OF WAR AND FAITH

I was raised by my Dad to have faith in God. Faith was not an option—it was our way of life. He would sit us around the kitchen table at night, with the youngest on his lap, and read from the Bible. Dad always made the stories come to life as he read to us; Dad was a very animated and humorous man. He could imitate every animal on Noah's ark. With our Dad, there was always a moral to the story. We learned much from our bonding time in the kitchen after supper. We missed those stories when he would have to go TDY for the air force, aka, temporary duty. He was always on alert, back in the sixties. Between Vietnam and the Cuban missile crisis and threats of invasions, he served his country. I was always very proud of my dad.

Then there was always my grandmother, my mom's mother. Both my dad and Memere made sure that we knew God; nightly prayers were part of our everyday lives. Memere is what we called her; she was very strict and yet full of love for her family. She's the same grandmother who cared for my brothers and me when my mom was hit by a car and unable to care for us.

I will always remember that day. I was just ten years old and I was home sick from school. My mom needed to go check the mail. She said to me, "Keep an eye on Timmy and I will be right back." Timmy was only a one-year-old. I loved my little brother—he was my real life doll. I played with him and took him for strolls in the big carriage. Time passed and mom had not come back; the mail was at the end of the street, so I could not visually see her. I was getting worried because she always came right back. Then I saw the neighbor run fast across my front yard and into my house. She said, "Your mom was hit by a car and she is in bad shape! The ambulance came and took her to the hospital! We need to call someone to take care of you kids."

"I will take care of my brothers," I said. "I know how to take care of my brothers! My mom taught me how to do all that. I can cook and do laundry." My mom had just made us matching dresses. "No one can take care of us! I can!"

The neighbor said, "We have to call the base; they will call the Red Cross and get your dad home." My dad was in Vietnam at this time. We were very close friends with our neighbors. My best friend was her daughter, and all the neighbors were military families. Military families have strong bonds for one another. I sometimes think the bonds are stronger than blood families.

One of our neighbors was a pilot. Every time he came home from a mission he would fly right over the house, and then we all knew Bob was home. He would BUZZ the houses with his F101 jet and we kids would all go running outside to see him fly over—that was such an awesome sight. He knew we would be excited, and his wife knew when to put the dinner on. My heart broke when I found out he had crashed his plane and had died as a hero, serving his country during the Vietnam War.

So, Dad is in Vietnam and Mom is being taken to the hospital. What a blur this was for a ten-year-old, but I was a mature ten-year-old. I could not believe my mom was hurt!

My uncle Ron, my mom's brother, was stationed at Woods Hole, Massachusetts. We lived in Falmouth at the time, right outside Otis Air Force Base. The neighbor called my uncle Ron; he was the nearest family member. He went right away to the ER to check on Mom. From what he said when he arrived, they had my mom on a stretcher in the hall. No one was helping her, and my uncle Ron was mad. He yelled, "Clean her up! Do something!" She was bleeding profusely from her head. Uncle Ron said he had never seen so much blood. She was given the last rites in the ER and again that night. The doctors were not sure whether she was going to live. Once the doctors stabilized her somewhat, she was transferred to Boston, to the Chelsea Naval Hospital.

The car that hit my mom did not see her crossing the road at first; when he did he tried to stop but could not. He hit her and she flew some thirty-five feet in the air and hit the ground. My mom had a broken arm, a broken pelvis, and multiple cuts and bruises. She also had a fractured skull and a concussion. Today she definitely would have been diagnosed with post-concussion syndrome: she had a very traumatic brain injury!

When she came to, the doctor in charge, who was an officer, said, "Shall we send for your husband? If he comes home now he will have to go back to Vietnam. He still has five months of time to do there and if he comes back now he will be over there for a longer time when he does go back." The doctor was suggesting that he serve his country first!

My mom, half in and out of consciousness, agreed; she wanted him home but she did not want him to go back. She was not fully functional; she was not mentally capable of making that choice. She was just coming out of surgery. There should have been no doubt. My dad was needed at home! The Red Cross said that he could not come home since he was in a war zone. There was no choice!

The neighbors took care of my brothers and me until my Memere could come. I was not leaving my house! The neighbors wanted us kids to come to their homes but I fought that one; I was the caregiver of my little brothers and I was very protective of them. I was the oldest of four; I had three younger brothers—Dean, a year younger than me; Phil, three years younger; and Timmy, eight years younger. It must have been sad for the neighbors to see a little girl trying to hold her family together at such a young age. My brothers and I were very frightened about what was going to happen to our family. The neighbors were talking about splitting us up and sending us to different homes.

My brothers and I missed our parents so much. My father told the story of calling to check on the family when he had an R&R in Japan. This is when he first found out about his wife being in a serious accident, and he tried to get back home. Dad said he flew from Tokyo to Saigon. He had a friend there named Pete. Pete was a good friend of our family; his wife and kids were living near us, again military kin. Pete told Dad he had a plane of news reporters going to Danang, and he could hop that flight. Dad got on that plane and said as they ascended upward off the airfield, he could clearly hear that something was wrong with the plane's engines. My dad was a plane man and he knew by the noise and the sputtering that something was definitely not right. He said he heard the noise and then all of a sudden they were heading downward fast. The plane crashed and by a miracle he got out alive. Only the people at the rear made it out.

He then caught a cargo plane. The troops needed supplies so my dad said he would help, if that would get him closer to going home. The plane was a C130. They approached the airfield; there were big potholes on the landing strip. They could hear the bullets hitting the plane! The pilot and crew said, "Open the bay and slide everything out; we have to get out of here! Our guys will get the supplies!" My dad said they pushed the supplies out as fast as they could. Dad said he was so scared for what was happening at home, and yet he also feared for his life in the middle of this war. When he reached Ankie, Vietnam, the Red Cross told him to go back. Go Back! My dad was so heartbroken because he wanted to come home! His wife and children needed him.

My brothers and I could not see my mom for three weeks, and when we finally saw her, she was black, blue, and purple. She had a cast on her arm and bandages everywhere—she was a mess! I hardly recognized her! She stayed in the hospital for six weeks, recovering. Then she needed full-time care at home. Thus began a long period of not having my parents at home. My grandmother took us to church, prayed with us, disciplined us, and loved us, but it was not the same as having your parents. We missed them so much.

We prayed every night for my parents, for one to be

healed and for both to come home. Looking back, we lost both parents that year; Mom was never the same. Dad was never the same either, when he finally came back from Vietnam. They divorced when I was twelve.

I grew up with faith. Faith in God. And faith in our country was vital, too. Right now at this broken stage of my life, I needed faith more than ever! I needed to show my own children more faith. I had always taken them to youth group, vacation Bible school, and church, and I prayed with them at night. But now I was standing on every inch of faith I had!

I had to find a job—a job that would pay me a man's wages. I am on guard to survive! Yet I am so broken! I found a job working at a call center for an auto parts plant. Before having children, I was a manufacturer's rep in the automotive aftermarket business. I know cars very well; I can even paint a car! I found a job requiring skills that I was familiar with and one that could make me enough money to support my family.

I was trained by another woman named Betsey; she was so kind to me—even when I cried and had to walk away from my training. I had a hard time concentrating. I told her about how hurt and broken I was; she also confided in me that she was unhappy with her husband. She sold stuff on eBay to make ends meet and worked full time. She wanted to leave him but had nowhere to go. I would have taken her in with her two children. I even told her that! After what I had been through, I did not want to hear of another woman suffering at all. I lived in a big Victorian house; I had a third-floor apartment she could have used. Everyone there was nice to me.

Even the manager would go for walks with me; when I cried at work he said, "One day he will be sorry and he'll find out the grass is not always greener on the other side."

The tears were for the divorce proceedings—I just filed the papers. I did not want to file, but had no choice. It felt like a death! Eddie was being so mean to me and the children. We had massive driveway confrontations! That is what I called it—"the driveway fights." He yelled at me and the kids; he would get up in my face and point his finger close to me! I was frightened! I would cry and stand still in shock!

"I am done with you!" he said, "It is your way or the highway! It's all about you! You always have to be right! You are ill! You are sick! Just get over it! Why do you always have to prove you are right! You're worthless, you're wasting my time, and I am going to find someone else! You're an alcoholic!"

Those were all his favorite things to say to me! They are still, to this day, etched in my mind and in the hearts of the children. My oldest could not believe what his step-dad was saying! My son wanted to punch Eddie, but I had raised him with respect, so that never happened. Some of the things Eddie said to me and about me sent me into a numbing state of feeling, like a zombie. The verbal assaults were unbelievable!

I would say to myself, where did that come from? That is not me. How could you think these things of me? He swore up and down that I was an alcoholic; he said this to everyone, all his friends, family. He had me believing I was a nothing! Yet I knew inside me I was a something. My heart sank to the pit of my stomach.

I would shake when Eddie came near me! He traumatized me! I felt he was a liar. I am not taking him to the cleaners, and I am not alienating his children. Words spread quickly in a small town. I would never do these things to anyone! I love my children!! He was alienating his own children and yet he could not see he ran us all off. My world is spinning! I am so confused. This is a man whom I married who is so cruel to me and the children, and no one can see it! "Oh, God, help me!" I would cry out every night. Why?

So much happened to the children on their visits that they did not want to go with him. He would drink and get drunk with his neighbors upstairs. The boys would say, "Mom, he was swaying and walking funny." He left them alone downstairs for hours, even though they were only ten! The children told me he took them to parties and did not pay attention to them. That sounded familiar! He could not pay attention to me, now he could not pay attention to them, either.

The stories the boys came home with bothered the hell out of me! What if something happened to them? They are still little kids!

The boys came home one Sunday night and said they were starving. I said, "Didn't your dad feed you?"

They said, "Only potato chips."

"Only potato chips? Why?" I said.

The boys said they were in a room all by themselves where there were no other children; dad was drinking that funny coke and beer downstairs, where the adults were at this birthday party. I said, "I am sorry, sweeties. Let's get something to eat." So I fed them some good food at nine at night and then put them to bed. They woke in the night throwing up potato chips; their stomachs hurt so badly. Stress, or bad chips, I do not know which it was. But he would not pay attention to them!

The boys are good kids! We have had a good way of life! I am a good mom! Why can't Eddie be a good dad to them? He would take them every Tuesday for two hours, but that schedule frequently changed. Sometimes it would be Wednesday, or Thursday, and every other weekend. But not all weekend! There were times he cancelled altogether on them. He would take them to his jobs sometimes on their visiting nights, and they would sit for hours while he worked. I thought, why didn't he work on the nights he did not have his children? I also wondered why this guy could not spend time alone with his own children. Were his friends more important? If he had his friends with him, Eddie would pay attention to whoever else was around, not his children. They wanted time alone with their dad! He just does not get it! It sure sounds familiar to me! I felt those kids' pain! Why could he not see their pain? My opinion is that Eddie wanted what Eddie wanted and NO ONE got in his way. I thought he was almost delusional about what he did to them. The boys would tell him they did not want to go to a party and he would say "TOO BAD—GET OVER IT! You will do what I say!" Once he grabbed Kevin by the leg, hard, when Kevin said he did not want to go. He was forcing them to do things that were uncomfortable to them. Kevin always fought back. He has a "stand up for justice" mentality, whereas Kyle is quiet, and does not like to make waves. But Eddie could not hear their cries and pleas…I thought it sounded so familiar, a duplicate of how he treated me; he could never hear my cries and pleas.

The children caught him lying, also. I was not surprised he called to cancel dinner one weeknight. He told the boys he had to work at a nearby store. So I told the boys, "Let's go out to the mall." So I took the back way. This route went right by where he was supposed to be working. I did not go that way on purpose because I had an errand to run before the mall. Well, his car was not there—no surprise. But to my utter surprise, we drove on our route to the mall and passed by the nearest popular bar, and the boys spoke up and said, "Look there is Dad's car!" I looked over and there was his car, not his work truck! The children were not surprised, but clearly they were angry at being lied to.

The boys have a friend, Bill, who lives on the other side of town; Kevin and Kyle would go to Bill's house a few nights each week. Bill's mom, Sheri, would pick the boys up and they did homework together while I was still at work. There were many nights and afternoons they saw their dad's car parked outside the local nationality club. It was a drinking club, the kind you have to belong to. How sad to see their dad there, mostly every day. I thought to myself, yeah right—I am the alcoholic, huh? When he left, I dumped all the booze down the sink. The children saw me pour bottle after bottle, even new ones, down the drain.

I had a hard time understanding and comprehending Eddie's behavior. I was terrified and scared of him, his mouth, and the look on his face when he yelled at me. Kyle even said, "Mom, Dad looks scary." So the children saw what I did; I am not imagining this. How sad for all of us. Eddie has screamed at me in the driveway in front of the kids, "I am not going to change, get over it."

I had dinner one night with Denise; we had a good heart-to-heart talk. We talked about how I was feeling and the trauma I experienced from Eddie's abusive ways. Denise said I should talk to a woman at the local Battered Women's

Shelter. That proved to be a big part of the healing I needed so badly—I needed to understand. I needed to understand what was happening to me. Why did Eddie treat me so badly? He never hit me, but his words and control cut into me like a knife. I was sliced into many pieces! Can I pick them up and put me back together? "Oh, God, help me pick up the pieces!" I would cry. I learned I was broken. My spirit was broken. My soul was severed.

A woman at the shelter saw me every time I went. Her name was Bobbie, and she was always there for me. She prayed with me; she was a spiritual woman. She tried to help me make sense out of what an emotional abuser can do to one's mind. Eddie was a big bully but at the same time he was a little man. Some of my friends thought I should be so lucky to have him as my husband. Underneath, I was slowly dying inside—a slow mental death!

Eddie was a big guy in the community. He was a hero, a fireman; he could hold someone's hand and tell them they were going to be fine. He could say to someone with confidence, "Hang on, and we can get you out of this car." He was, in a way, almost obsessive about being at the scene when all the scanners went off, being at each and every big fire, car accident, anything happening in our small city. He was only a call fireman—not a lifer. I saw him act compulsively, like he would feel left out if he was not there when the scanners went off.

What about us? What about your family? You are not emotionally there for us! But what a big bully he is—why? I have only known one other bully—on the playground in elementary school. Wow, I married one!

I learned so much from being counseled at the shelter; I thank God for putting Bobbie in my path. And Denise always came to my rescue; I am so thankful for the friends I have.

Eddie said I have no friends because I am ill! I have lots of friends now—good ones. Even most of my old neighbors! Neighbors see everything! Kay could see how he interrupted me when I spoke, how he would exclude me from conversations. Even if I left the room because I felt like a nothing, Kay would try to come with me. He would draw her back into the conversation, preventing her from following me! Kay saw this happening; she told me only after Eddie had moved out, when I told her my heartaches. She is my sister in this world, even though I never had a real sister. I have lots of sisters at church, I have friends at work, and I have friends in California. I have friends, just not his kind of friends.

My children will have their own war and faith to bear, just as I did—different war, same faith.

CHAPTER 6
THE CONFESSION

The war was being fought, unbeknownst to me. I was frightened of what was to become of the children and myself. There was no reasoning with Eddie. Even the children tried to talk to him; he would tell them again and again, "Get over it!" Both the children and myself were under attack by Eddie. The bully he is was horrific for us—he had no mercy. He could not even be nice. He was losing his own children but he could not see this. But everything was my fault. Right!

I tried so hard to talk and reason with him. I even gave him a book that showed him what was wrong with him and us as a family. The book is called *The Verbally Abusive Relationship*, by Patricia Evans. This book was helping me understand many, many things; Eddie would spout horrible things at me, then not remember saying them. Some of the things he would say sent me into shock mode. He would say,

"I never said that." He did this constantly to me. It drove me crazy!

Even simple things became a problem: I would ask him to please be home by six o'clock. He would then arrive home at seven and say I'd never told him what time to be home. He would always get mad if I challenged him. What was truth, or and what was a lie? This type of abuse is called "crazy-making." I constantly felt like I was confused and an enemy in our relationship. What is really odd is he tells people I am crazy!

I really hoped Eddie would look at *The Verbally Abusive Relationship*, and I prayed he could see what I saw in this book. In my opinion, Eddie is a manipulator and the type of verbal abuser that is harmful to the mind and to the soul. Eddie discounted me as a person.

"Discounting denies the reality and experience of the partner and is extremely destructive. If the partner does not recognize it for what it is, she may spend years trying to figure out what is wrong with her ability to communicate. Discounting denies and distorts the partner's actual perception of the abuse and is, therefore, one of the most insidious forms of abuse" (Patricia Evans, *The Verbally Abusive Relationship*, p. 91).

If only some kind of lightbulb turned on in Eddie, maybe he could change. Bobbie, at the shelter, was teaching me to cope; Eddie was just so cruel. He did not care what the children and I had to say, he did not care what Pastor was telling him either, and Pastor told me so.

I wrote a long e-mail to Eddie, which took me all day to write; I shed many tears over it. It was a very important e-mail; it was giving him a chance to get help. He read it and never responded; this message could have been his ticket home. I did ask if he got the message and he said yes. He said nothing; it was not important to him. The message was about abuse, healing, forgiveness, and God. He did not care! That's when I knew I had to file for divorce. The hurts ran deep; he made me and the children miserable.

I have no regrets—we needed peace. I know my spiritual inner voice said he had to go, but I had prayed Eddie would wake up and miss us and want to make it all right. Eddie knew this; he knew how I felt. I remember him one time screaming in my face, "Didn't work out like you planned, huh, Amy!" He knew! He knew I wanted him to change. He said, "I am not going to change—get over it!"

Here I am working all day now, trying to function. I had a quota to meet; the goals were set at the call center. In six months I would go on full commission only; first, I had to build a customer base. Both Dave and I started at the same time; he had a family to support also.

During Thanksgiving, a got pneumonia and was very sick. Every Thanksgiving the children and I had always spent the day with the veterans. Eddie always volunteered to work the holidays at the fire station. I swear, Eddie hated to be home. I had decided to show the kids how to serve others; I was actually on the board of directors of our local veterans' outreach center. I was happy to serve; I learned much about PTSD and veterans' affairs. My poor dad was living a hell, and I had no idea how to help him. I felt if I got involved I could make a difference. The children enjoyed those Thanksgivings; they played checkers and even learned how to do wood burning from one of the veterans.

This Thanksgiving I could not bring them; I told them I was too sick to go. I was a mess; I had a high fever and was so weak I could not even get up. I called Eddie and asked him to please come over and feed them since I could not. The church dropped us off a Thanksgiving basket—I was so thankful. I could not even go shopping I was so sick. Eddie did come over that day and made dinner; I had managed to put the turkey in the oven for him. So the turkey was cooked and I thought he would spend time with the children on Thanksgiving.

I could not believe what he did after dinner: he came into the living room and passed out on the recliner and spent no time with his children. Here I am, sick enough that I should be in the hospital, and he comes in and passes out. Why was he so comfortable? I thought, he was not normal today. I prayed he would come to his senses; he woke up in the darkness of the evening and said good-bye to the children and left. Not one word was said to me. What an empty feeling that was. I was disregarded, a nothing, as usual. I thought, was it just his duty to make sure the children had some kind of dinner? And that was it.

I did start to recover from the pneumonia and went back to work. I was off for a few weeks. I went back and tried to work but my first commission check was only about eighty dollars. Dave earned about the same, and he quit. He had to move on and support his family. I tried another few weeks but the commission was not good.

I thought I could make more money by selling cars. So that is what I did; I went to work at a dealership selling trucks. It was a mindless job but it was hard work—fifty-plus hours a week, including weekends. I thought to myself, this was too much. Is this what it comes down to? How am I going to support myself and the children? They deserved better than this.

The divorce proceedings were going along slowly. It was hell on earth. I could not believe he would actually go full steam ahead with trying to give me nothing from a fifteen-year marriage. I just wanted my children. That was all I cared about. They were my life and my responsibility to God to raise. I filed for cruel and abusive reasons. When we went to court, I was petrified of what Eddie was going to do to me. The real kicker here is that with him being a big fireman, he called the local state representative to be his lawyer. He got out the big guns to get me.

"Oh, my God," I cried. I knew this state rep; he had helped my grandmother with a new law for blind people. My grandmother needed benefits and he helped. He even took her to the state house. I also knew him from the veterans' center. He helped get our funding and grants. I thought to myself, he should know my character, shouldn't he?

Now here is State Representative Alex Kane talking badly about me during mediation. He called me an alcoholic! And he said what I was doing to the children was wrong—turning them against their dad.

I went into shock mode—I was in disbelief of what was being said. This was wrong and this was not registering in by brain. I was under attack by Eddie, legally now! He was using his lawyer to launch his assaults. But how could Alex think this of me? I looked at his face and it was red.

It was a show! I could tell by his face, it was a show.

I grabbed my lawyer's arm; I looked at Alex and said, "How could you judge me—you do not even know me."

My lawyer called for a break. We went outside and he said, "Amy, this is a show for his client."

I told my lawyer, "I know what Eddie was getting at; he wanted to show me up to be an alcoholic so he could take the children, and he also wanted to show that I was turning his kids against their dad."

"Oh, my God!" I was so shocked. I was shaking horribly inside. My head hurt so badly, my stomach was sick. I have lost so much weight from all this, and the lies are getting deeper. How can I prove I am not doing these things? Eddie will try and convince the courts. I know him! I know him!

"I just want my children," I told my lawyer. He understood what to do. I did not care about the money—Eddie is pushing to have it all. I would receive no pension, no 401k; he wanted me to have nothing. That included the children. He was not going to stop until he got what he wanted, just as he promised the day he moved out—"By the time I am through with you, you will have no house, no car, no kids, and no nothing." He was really going to make good on this. In my shock, I was mad. What did I ever do to him to deserve this type of insanity? "Why?" I asked myself, "What is wrong with him?" I was a good wife and mother. We did both drink at parties, and I could not handle alcohol. I was not good with the stuff, but it did numb my pain—the pain I endured from a husband who was unavailable and confusing.

I knew before the Jimmy Buffet concert that I hated drinking, and I did not want to do it anymore. Something bad happened at my oldest son's graduation a few months before the concert. I planned his party, I made all the food, and rented a hall for the family to come and celebrate. When people came, Eddie stayed at the bar and continued to drink all day and ignored the children and myself. He was laughing and having a grand old time with all the men's type of men. It was like a picture I have seen for many, many years at any function we went to.

I was making sure to keep up with the food supply and trying to stay connected with our friends. Some who did not drink witnessed what I saw in Eddie. His family only saw me acting upset, as always. After the party was ending and my good friends had left, the drinkers were still there. I thought I could have a few drinks with them. A couple of them were friends I have known for a while. I used to be able to party with them, but lately I wanted to be with my friends who could laugh and be mature—or was it that I needed something spiritual? I was growing up, or something was changing in me. I did not want to party. I did have a few drinks and then I seemed to just snap. I wanted to go home—I was feeling very wasted. I did not drink that much, but something did not feel right! I wanted to go home, and I became increasingly stubborn; I left and wanted to walk home. I know I needed to walk it off. Because something did not feel right, I did just that—I started to walk. I knew my way home and I thought I would feel better when I got there.

I was walking, and I was halfway home when the police pulled up and said Eddie had called them to pick me up and bring me home.

I was so embarrassed; I wanted to walk home. The police said if I did not get in the car they would take me to the station forcibly. I got in but I was scared to go home; I was crying so hard. I could not believe Eddie would do this to me. I could not believe that I was in the back of a police cruiser. I felt like I had done something bad. I was very shaken and scared by this experience, and upset. I told the police, "Please do not take me home. Bring me to my neighbor's house; they will take me in." I was afraid of Eddie. Thank God they brought me to the neighbor's house.

I called my cousin Rick. He came and got me and we hung out for a while. I told my cousin how I felt; I must have sounded like something out of a chick flick. Eddie was playing these intense mind games with me; he must have sounded like this great husband and father, but in our home we were all miserable. We wanted him to change. I wanted him to change. If I did anything wrong, anything at all, Eddie made it out like I had committed the worst crime ever. He would take something small and blow it up into something big. I did everything wrong. I told Rick I could not take much more. It was all so crazy. Eddie did not really care for Rick as he was not his type, but I felt safe with Rick, and I trusted him.

I told Rick maybe he could go in first, and make sure it was okay for me to go home. He said, "Okay", and then he took me home.

The lights were on and Eddie was waiting for me. I just knew it. Rick went to the door and talked to Eddie for a few moments. Rick came back to his truck and he said, "I cannot believe what he just said to me."

Eddie said, "I believe you have something that belongs to me."

Rick said, "If you are talking about my cousin, she wants to come in, and she is not a thing." Rick was not happy and told me, "He treats you like a possession!" Yes! My cousin saw it too! I am not crazy!

Rick said, "It is okay; call me if you need me." I thanked him and gave him a hug good-bye.

I went into my home and I was afraid. Eddie had verbally attacked me about being an alcoholic and how bad I was and how I had acted like an idiot. I felt like a child who had done nothing wrong but was getting the blame. I went to bed. When I got up the next day I was too embarrassed to see anyone. I did not want to see anyone. I wanted to isolate myself and never come out. I felt humiliated and tricked by Eddie. I swear, he did anything to make me feel bad and on guard. I needed to stay home and be quiet.

I did call my friend Sue and told her what happened after I left the party. I asked her what happened; I could not remember! I told her I just did not feel right. She told me something that sent shock waves to my soul. She said, "The bartender was spiking your drinks." She and others said, "The mother of the graduate should have some fun, also." I was hostess to my son's party and worked hard to have a nice party for him. The mom needed to have fun?

They all knew? I had no idea of how much I drank. This is a nightmare come true. Who would do such a thing? I wanted to call the police and report the bar. But of course I would look like I am as crazy as Eddie makes me. It would be their word against mine. And who would want to shut this club down; there are too many politics at this place. That bartender could have killed me!

I thought if I did call, Eddie would have said, "See, I told you all about her. She is crazy and an alcoholic." My life was reeling out of control, my mind was on alert, and my body was on alert. I was afraid of him. Why can't he see? I am a good person! I am not an alcoholic. I asked myself today, "What else did someone put in my drink?"

I understand full well and I told my lawyer what Eddie

is up to. I begged my lawyer to help me. I know Eddie all to well. He has this puppy-dog look that everyone believes. I cannot lose my children. I had been a stay-at-home mom up until three years ago. I was the type of mom who had a garden and made jam. Neighborhood kids loved my home; I was the mom of moms! I am now working hard to maintain forty-plus hours and take care of the children. I have asked Eddie to help me; he says he cannot help me because he has to work. I have to work, too.

If the children get sick I have to leave my job and take care of them. I do not mind, but help would be nice. My employer was getting a bit upset about my taking time off. I begged Eddie to help because Emily was getting really sick lately and needed more medical attention, and the boys were acting up after school.

The boys had not wanted to go with him—I wonder why? I had my hands full; Eddie could only say to me, "Quit complaining. If you cannot handle the children, I will take them off your hands." I was speechless, shocked, and mortified! I thought to myself, these are your children—not weapons to use against me, to make me fail as a parent. He was choking me the best way he could: by not helping, not giving nor wanting to give us any money. I say "us" because he was doing this to the children. I saw they were losing their respect for their dad.

He took Kevin and Kyle to Wal-Mart. They told me that they asked him for a pack of gum, which cost ten cents.

He said, "No, I give your mom all my money and I have only five dollars left when I am done." Then, right in front of them, he buys a DVD boxed set of the "Rescue Me" TV series—for eighty dollars!!

The boys have never forgotten that—they are children but they are not stupid. I could see that he was playing mind games with them! I thought, oh, my, can you believe this is his way of life?

Well, the war that was previously unknown to me was just beginning. Eddie is out for my throat. Why someone would be so vengeful is beyond me. He is slandering my name through our town; friends have told me that they think there is no need of this childish behavior.

My lawyer's name is Gerry Taylor; he is a kind man. And he knows the type of person Eddie is. Even though he is such a good lawyer, he is having trouble handling a bully like Eddie. Gerry is a family man, a just man; he does everything by the book. He will not play Eddie's games; he will serve me in the way the court asks.

Thus began a big mind game of lies and deceit.

Eddie had worked at a company called AllRight Services in a service industry since he got out of high school; it was owned by a distant relative. So, when Eddie decided to become a full-time fireman, we agreed he could do both. The fire department was a two-day deal. He had five other days to work. Almost all firemen have side businesses. He made more money on the business than from being a fireman. Eddie was making quite a bit of money. That is why I could stay home and raise the children.

He had been an army national guardsman for years and still worked for AllRight Services. So when he wanted to work for our city, we decided to start our own business doing what he did since graduating from high school—the same type of business as AllRight Services. We bought our own truck and he had lots of tools. That used to be a sore spot with me; when I was coupon-clipping: he spent two hundred dollars a month on tools, and then some. That amount of money could have bought a lot of food for our family, but he was in charge of "his money." So we built a business, for many years.

When the divorce agreement was being discussed, Eddie's lawyer announced in the court papers that Eddie was going to be just a fireman and that was all. He said that Eddie wanted to spend more time with his three growing children. He listed the worth of his business at $950.00. He did this so I would get practically no child support. And according to the state guidelines, he was paying what was needed to support them. Between the fire department and his business, we would lose so much support if we had only the money from his salary as a fireman.

Then his lawyer said to me and my lawyer, "Never mind the cruel and abusive claim; let's just get these two people divorced!" I wanted the cruel and abusive claim in my court papers; his lawyer just scribbled it off the papers for court! Then he proceeded to sit back down in the courtroom. I stood there speechless, feeling sick to my stomach. I was under so much duress from being bombarded by bullies. He scribbled it off! It did not matter to him; I was an invisible thing and did not matter. Eddie has hurt my total being and it just does not matter to him or anyone!

I was in shock in the courthouse; I saw the woman judge being taken in by this fireman and by the state rep standing in front of her. She was in favor of Eddie just having one job. No man should work more then forty hours. He was to sell the business, we were to sell our home, and be on our way.

We could not agree, I could not agree! Can you imagine? He was doing just what he said he would do to me and he was getting away with it! In my opinion, this judge was for the man! By law, I had to walk away with some kind of equity. He also stated I was unstable with my job situation. His lawyer made me sound like I could not hold a job. He was setting me up to look unstable! My God! I had been a stay-at-home mom for many years; I did not know what I wanted to do. My career was my children! My lawyer was not a scum lawyer; he did not work in the same manner Eddie's was working; I had to fight for myself!

I was frantic to try and prove the business was worth a lot more than $950.00. I went home and sat down in our office and started going through all the paperwork we had on his business. Good thing I did not let him take that paperwork when he left. I found files of tools and equipment totaling about $30,000 worth, plus! And I could produce more!

I also found a file that made me sick. The file contained many years of our dish television sales invoices; he had paid per automatic debit. He had stapled the bills shut every month. I opened them and to my surprise our bills were between, $100 to $250 a month! He was paying for pornographic channels! I took all these bills from my hand and scattered them across the floor, and I cried. I also found bills from a credit card stapled together, like he was hiding it, like he could staple something shut and it would not surface. These bills were from an Internet site for $39.00 per month. He had bought a new laptop for his business; he was always working on it for his business. He did a lot of work at the fire station also on that laptop! Wow, I thought to myself, he even had a portable way to watch it.

I had caught him a few times viewing porn, but I did not know it was to this extent! In my opinion, men who are obsessed with porn love to be with themselves, and that is what he did during our whole marriage. He loved on himself! No wonder why I felt the way I did. I knew I felt for many years he was unemotional toward me.

The vision came to me at the concert when he was watching the women with no shirts on; the whole scene of the concert now came running back into my mind. Porn hurts families! When you can turn a woman off with a remote you have big issues! The times he viewed were right after I had gone to bed. He said he just had to watch the weather and then he'd be right up to bed. Thus, he came in at all hours of the night—slamming doors and scaring me to death, for years. He would say "Oh, honey, I am sorry I fell asleep watching the weather." How many years did I hear that excuse? Once I was pregnant with Emily, I felt he was done with me! I felt like I was not the "hot woman" anymore. God knows I tried to please him. I was beating a dead horse for far too many years. What was wrong with this picture?

I went to see my pastor. I had to tell him everything—I was so upset and confused. Pastor did not like one bit of what Eddie was doing to the children and me. In a sense, Pastor said, "By church standards Eddie deserted us." I could tell by Pastor's face he knew far more than he could say, but I could tell he was sickened by Eddie.

Then, Pastor said, "Eddie has something important to tell you. You need to see him and ask him." Pastor smiled, like he was relieved for me. I prayed that smile was for the good.

I called Eddie and he said he would come by the house that night. I thought to myself, maybe he has a deep dark secret that he was molested as a young man and knew he needed help. I really thought that this would be a good explanation because of the way he was toward me. I thought he could get help and we could work though this—maybe that is why he was so angry and had temper tantrums. He treated me with no respect, but I am okay. He will be okay.

Eddie came and we sat in the car—another driveway moment. I told him I had talked to Pastor and I knew he had been meeting with him lately. "Pastor said you have something important to tell me," I stated. We sat in my car and he confessed that he had sex on the party bus. I was floored—stunned, you could say. That is not the answer I expected. I was quiet for a moment and thought, "He has been mad at himself."

I said, "With whom?"

He said, "I do not know who."

I said, "I cannot believe that! You do not have sex with a woman and say she is quiet! How stupid do you think I am?"

He told me he went into the concert; at that time he felt bad that I had left. His buddy was busy in the emergency tent, so he just went back to sit on the bus alone. He did not feel right at that point that I was not there. Then there was a woman in the dark, and she just came over and wanted oral sex. And that was it.

I said, "I am sorry, but I cannot believe that nothing was spoken between two people engaged in sex."

My brain was on overdrive; I was confused by the answer he gave me. After listening to Eddie's story, I could not believe what he had said. Then it clicked in my brain: I felt that somehow it sounded like he was justifying his behavior. Just like when he said to me, "It was just a little wet T-shirt contest." Like I was overexaggerating as usual! I saw a sick man that day! No one else saw, just me and my God.

He told me, "Now you can have the divorce you deserve." According to God, a woman who divorces her husband by church standards shall not marry again unless adultery is involved. And guess what—he did it—he cheated and committed the sin of adultery. I had NEVER cheated on him, ever. There were a few times his friends told me to leave him; a few of them even made passes at me. But NEVER did I cross any lines. One of his good friends really cared for me, and it felt good to have attention, but I was committed to my marriage—good or bad.

There were a few times in my marriage that I felt tempted, especially when I really needed to feel human and wanted attention. I needed to feel attractive and sometimes the attention was nice. I would go out with my girlfriends sometimes and flirt. However, I never ever crossed that line—tempted, yes, but never unfaithful. My friend and old neighbor told me, "Amy, in marriage there are many hills, mountains, valleys, and flat plains. You have to ride them out and hang on for dear life." I have seen her do that in her marriage; I admire her for her commitment.

Finally, Eddie said, "I am done with you!"

In such desperation to make things right, I told him I could forgive him.

He said, "Too Bad, Amy—get over it." How could he just walk away from his own sins? I wanted him to get help, but he wanted no part of it.

So guilt is a heavy burden, but I guess confession is good for the soul.

CHAPTER 7
THE EDDIE HASKELL SYNDROME

I was hurt; I was confused and very numb. I must have looked like a deer by the side of the road, the one that stares at the headlights. It does not move—it just stares at the headlights, frozen—frozen in shock and horror of an unknown bright light—blinding it into stillness.

As for me, I know I have Post Traumatic Stress Disorder. I have symptoms off the map. The accident was bad enough, but what Eddie has done to me emotionally—I feel like he is trying to do me in with the mind games, vengefulness, and lies. I question myself about what is next—I feel he is unstoppable when he wants something. I remember years ago how he acted when he wanted me.

In my opinion, he has the same charms as did the character Eddie Haskell on the TV show, *Leave it to Beaver*. You can still watch the reruns on TV Land. I watched that show when I was a kid. Wally and Beaver always fell for Eddie

Haskell's crazy-making ways. Eddie charmed the heck out of Mrs. Cleaver, Wally's and Beaver's mom. It seemed that Eddie Haskell could do no wrong; I think Eddie Howard was molded after Eddie Haskell. He never looks you in the eye, and always has the innocent puppy-dog look on his face. He gets what he wants—always—then he casts aside the people who are suppose to matter. In my case, I felt the children and I were reduced to redundancies.

Whenever I think of my situation, my chest hurts from the adrenaline flowing through my body and from my heart beating so fast. My stomach hurts, but my headache is unbearable. So much is happening, I want to stay in my bed and never get out of it. With every inch of me, the person that I am inside my wounded self, I know I have my children to love and to take care of.

With all the working and coping in my life to deal with right now, on top of everything else, my grandfather was dying. My last living grandfather—the one who taught me all about cars, the one who used to make Memere all upset. She would say to me, "You do not need to know about cars! That is a man's work." No one could keep me from sneaking in there to see him hoist an engine up on the pulley so he could take it all apart to make it run better, and maybe faster.

All of my uncles, my mom's brothers, had fast cars and they were always at my grandfather's garage. My uncle Derik had the fastest 1964 red Ford Fairlane convertible around. Derik would take my brothers and me for rides around the back roads of New England, singing Beach Boys' songs. Seems funny that today my brother Timmy owns a 1964 fully restored GTO. The car stuff ran deep in my family's veins, even though Memere said that car stuff was not for a girl.

Eddie had even bought me a fortieth birthday present. It was a muscle car, a 1938 Ford Coupe, but I never got to drive it. He bought it the day after my accident, but my neck and back were so hurt I could not use the manual steering. I believe he really bought it for himself, not me. The year of my fortieth birthday was a blur; nothing was right in my world.

My grandfather, Pepere, as we called him, was very sick and in the nursing home. My Memere, Mom, and Kenny, a friend of the family, tried to take care of him at home for a long time. Pepere just got so weak he did not want to eat; all he did was sleep. He finally fell out of bed. His body was so tired; he also had a bad bed sore that became abscessed and it had to be taken care of; he was in much pain from it. They could no longer care for him at home, and so he went into the nursing home. The home was close to us so we could visit him daily. Slowly he succumbed to his death, breathing his last breaths with a little help from the morphine. He did make it to his ninetieth birthday; I hated to see him go. It was so sad; the children loved him so much. He was the only great-grandfather they ever knew.

While I was coping with the loss of my grandfather's death, not one hour after the nursing home called the funeral parlor, Eddie called me and said, "Sorry for your loss."

Oh, my God—I am in shock, how did he know? It was not even announced yet! How could he be sorry? He did not even like my grandfather! He never once came to see him in the nursing home, not once. I felt like it was his way to invade my privacy! I was astonished at this phone call. Eddie then said, "The funeral director called and told me." I was so mad! I thought the director had no right to do that. None.

But then, he was Eddie's friend. I was shaking when he told me; the director was the one who had hired the bus to the Jimmy Buffett concert. His wife was involved with the wet T-shirt contest, and a few of the men who worked at the funeral home were on the bus. The band of brothers are all men's men. My insides were screaming with panic and fear. My heart was beating out of my chest. I cried—I had to face these people.

Then Eddie said, "I want to come to the funeral for the children; I want to be there for them." I hung up on him. I was breathless and felt invaded; he wanted to be there for the children? I thought, he is not there for them daily, or even as a father. I was stunned, shocked, and sick to my stomach.

I called my lawyer right away. I told my lawyer, "My family and I do not want him there. This is about my grandfather's passing. It's not about Eddie's social status and missing out on a social gathering. My children and I are there for each other."

I was appalled! I felt that if something ever happened in his family and one of them died, his two sisters and mom would have me burned at the stake if I attended. My lawyer called Eddie's lawyer and told him Eddie was not wanted at the funeral and it was not his place to go, considering the circumstances. I thought, he just did not have a clue, or was he tormenting me on purpose?

It was bad enough to have to bury my grandfather, but I had to walk with my head up past these men at the funeral parlor. I was proud of Emily that day. She did a Bible reading and brought the gifts of communion for our Pepere's funeral. All my cousins were there. Though it was sad, it was nice to see my family all gathered.

At this point I am so glad I have my family; I just wish my friend and cousin, Sally, lived closer. Even though she lives in Michigan, every time we are together we are inseparable. We are so much alike; I wish we could visit more often. We laugh like teenagers together. We do the sleepover thing. I cry every time she goes home.

So, in the midst of Eddie's chaotic whirlwind of craziness, I found some sanity in seeing my family drawn together.

As we left the church after the funeral, the funeral director looked at me and said, "I wish you luck. You're going to need it."

I knew he meant about divorcing Eddie, but how did he mean it? I wonder if he knew how vengeful Eddie was toward me? I wondered if he was a good and just man and he knew what was coming at me? I really wondered if he only knew the whole story, the real story. I really doubt that he did because he did not live behind my four walls—no one did. I am not crazy, I am a good person; I remember me before Eddie. I am still in there somewhere. I wish he could see my heart; I wish someone would.

Now we have a holiday coming up—Easter—and I got an invitation to go to Kay's house.

Kay called and said, "You really need to come and get away from all the mess there." The kids all missed each other and I think she was worried about me. She had every reason to worry—I was a mess. I told her I would come. I got the car packed; the kids were ready and excited. It was going to be an eight-hour drive yet I felt so numb. I wanted to go, yet I was spazzing out: PMS time. I felt empty inside and felt empty leaving home; I felt very confused.

I went by my Memere's house before I left town. I told the children to wait in the car, as I needed to calm down and connect to someone I knew who loved me. I went into the house and ran into my grandmother's, arms and sobbed like someone who had just lost her best friend. My grandmother held me and let me cry and then she prayed for me. She prayed for peace for my soul. Even with all the madness of Eddie, I needed peace, and to feel like I was okay: I was sane, and I was loved. Memere loved me always, since the day I was born, and she loved my children. She loved her family more than anything else in the world. She came to all of her granddaughters' homes when we each had our first child; she had to make sure we would be okay to take care of our babies. She taught us what we did not know naturally. She was the best grandmother, and here she had just lost her husband last month. She knew pain, and yet she knew love.

So off we went, the children and I, to Kay's house. Kay and John had been our neighbors for about eight years. Danny actually used to babysit Kay's boys, Mark and Sean. We were all very close. We raised our children together. I can still see those kids all running home from school, like they just could not get home fast enough. We spent birthdays and Sunday BBQs together.

After they moved away, Kay and I stayed close. I know John did talk to Eddie now and then. But I try to stay away from that subject, and I am careful about what I say to John, for fear of Eddie coming back at me for something I might have said and twisting it, as always. There was a lot of that going on; I really did not know whom to trust. I did not want to lose my children. I really stayed to myself, especially because of this court battle that was going on and because of the consequences of the mind games, in my opinion, of his narcissistic-type personality.

Eddie tells me things like, "Even your own family thinks you are crazy. There are plenty of people who think you are out of your mind!"

I will stand strong with his insults and badgering, but it hurts like hell, and I doubt myself so much.

We drove to Kay's house and pulled in around suppertime—it felt like old home week. They are like family to the kids and me. We had dinner and watched some movies. The next day, John had the kids flying kites in the yard. They were all laughing and having a good time. All five boys were together. They really could all be brothers—they even laughed alike. Kay, Emily, and I went for a walk around the neighborhood. It was a beautiful April day—a little windy, but beautiful. We went in and had lunch, Kay had made BBQ sandwiches that were to die for!

The kids scattered after lunch to play games and watch movies in the family room downstairs, and we adults set up camp upstairs. John had rented us a chick flick, being the good husband. I know they were trying to cheer me up; John had rented *Under the Tuscan Sun* with Diane Lane. We started watching it; in the beginning, Diane Lane is going through a divorce and it is so not pleasant. Well, I began to cry, noticeably crying; poor John paused the movie and said, "We can change this movie."

Through my tears I said, "I wanted to watch it—I will be okay." After the movie, John said something to me that has stuck with me till this day. He looked at me and said, "Amy, he is so not worth your tears."

I said, "I know, John, but it still hurts." I know in my heart, John knew more than he could say. But I respected him so much for that comment. John himself was raised by a single mom who prevailed and raised his sister and him very well; they worked hard to preserve their family. John knew that was where I was coming from—it was all about family.

Over the long weekend, we had Easter dinner together and celebrated Danny's birthday. I know I repeated myself a lot to Kay and John, but I was in such a numb-feeling mode of what was reality and what was distorted.

Too soon it was time to head back home. We promised to come back soon. Kay does come to our town with the kids off and on, as her family all lives here. Plus, we talk daily; she has listened and been the best friend ever. I do not know how she has put up with me; I cry so much that it is unbelievable. But she is there, and I am so thankful for her insight and friendship.

As I drive back home I am thinking to myself—time to go back to reality and the war zone. Lord knows what I face next. I could feel in the pit of my stomach that I did not want to know.

I was still selling cars, but I had changed dealerships. I liked this dealership much better. They really wanted women working for them so there were about five of us. That part was great, but the hours were long and tiring.

To this day, I wonder how we all managed to pull together as a family. The older two helped with Kevin and Kyle, getting them to bed when I worked late. Looking back, they knew it was vital that we needed to support each other because everything was changing. There was such an unknown feeling between all of us. A silent war for survival was being fought.

It was Eddie's weekend with the children; he picked

them up Friday night and brought Emily back before bed. She hated to sleep anywhere but her own bed—she always has been that way. She loved her home; it was her safe place. Kevin and Kyle went back with him to his apartment. I worried so much about them, with Eddie drinking upstairs and coming home looped. It scared me for their safety. Every weekend I worried.

Lydia, my neighbor across the street, came over. We had a fire in the *chiminea*, my Mexican outdoor fireplace, and a glass of wine. It was a beautiful cool night—great for a warm fire. Every neighbor I have ever had has been the best. I have special bonds with my neighbor girlfriends. Lydia was a teacher and she loved my children. She was like me in basic ways: we were moms, and homebodies. You would have to meet her to see what a special person she is, the type that has charisma and truly cares for people. Lydia went through a terrible divorce years ago and waited a long time to remarry. She met and married Jeff a couple summers ago; they are definitely soul mates. They were kind of like the Brady Bunch on TV: they both had children from previous marriages. They juggled and their home was full.

Lydia is realistic about life, and what is good, and what is evil. She is a Christian and her light shines in her way of living and thinking. Lydia told me she hated to see what Eddie was putting me and the kids through. Tonight she could not contain herself. I had been crying, worrying about the children, and wondering why Eddie was doing this to me, to us.

Lydia said to me, "Amy, please stop crying. He is so not worth those tears. Eddie came by the house the other night and embarrassed my husband by the way he was talking. Jeff's face turned all three shades of red, when Eddie started bragging about the women he is hanging out with and what they are doing sexually. Amy, please stop wasting your tears on this guy. He is acting like a teenager."

I respected her even more for being truthful. Eddie has not missed a beat; he is out messing around. Her words were close to what John told me, "He is not worth your tears."

The wife of another friend of Eddie's told me Eddie cannot wait till he can be seen in public with his new girl-friend, instead of hiding out. In my opinion, I do believe he had a girlfriend all along, or many. But to my family he said about me, "I loved her so much." I felt like: Liar, Liar.

I realized that Eddie thought I was no different from his ex-girlfriends. The reality is I thought I was different especially because he married me. I do remember two of his ex-girlfriends, one who acted out on his unavailability—I saw her. She flirted with all the men in sight to get him to pay attention to her. She was called a whore by Eddie. Today I feel bad for her, but I bet she would feel worse for me because I married him. Then there was the girlfriend before me. She had him in counseling because he could not seem to come home enough and be with her—he told me so. Does this all sound to familiar? RED FLAGS! I should have seen them all!

In my opinion, he charmed them, used them, and then cast them aside. They were nothings, like me. He even bought the last one brand- new furniture from the big furniture store in Framingham. He left her with all new appliances, TVs—you name it. I had always wondered why he had nothing when I met him—only a bag of clothes and no credit. I think back now and realized that something bad could have happened with her when he was done with her. Then I rescued him from her. More RED FLAGS I did not see!

I really thought he had the Eddie Haskell syndrome—he was so nice, and nothing was ever his fault. It was them, I thought to myself—a whore, and a cling-on. But I am so lucky: I am called a whore, a cling-on, and a crazy alcoholic to my face! At the end of their relationships with Eddie, they also must have felt the way I did. I have never met anyone like this in my life. I trusted him with my heart, as they must have; I felt he broke this trust like we were nothings. He opens doors, takes you to dinner and lots of weekend trips; you are a queen.

As Eddie Haskell would say, "Thank you, Mrs. Cleaver, but I must go. Is there anything else I can do for you, Mrs. Cleaver?"

CHAPTER 8
CRAZY-MAKING;
"THEY ARE MORE AFRAID OF YOU, THAN ME!"

O h, the charms of Eddie—he picked up the boys for their weekly dinner night and now Dad has another new friend. Her name is Vicky. The boys came home and told me all about it, all by themselves.

"Mom," they said, "we went to Vicky's house and watched a movie, while dad was upstairs in the bedroom. He said he was fixing the vacuum cleaner. We had to go find him when the movie was done."

I thought to myself, Lydia was right: he has moved on, not only the woman on the bus and the others he was bragging about, but now we have Vicky. And we are not even divorced! I thought, oh, my, to bring the children into this situation now is not right.

According to the children, he left them in a new place, unattended for hours. I was thinking to myself: this is your night with them! Fixing a vacuum cleaner upstairs in a bed-room, I thought, wasn't that quite odd?

So began the relationship with Vicky. This was Dad's new friend and that is all the boys took it for, a new friend. But they caught on real quick; Eddie was picking them up now on his scheduled times. But Vicky was always there. They never had just "Dad time," and they were getting upset. And they told him so,

The boys would say, "It is just us tonight, right, Dad?"

He would say, "Yes." Then, when they got into the car, he would call her on the phone right in front of them, and tell her where to meet them, and which restaurant. The children said they did not trust him; they felt tricked. They kept getting angry. Or they would come home and say Vicky just happened to show up where we were.

The poor kids felt they were ignored while he paid attention to Vicky. One week, Eddie asked my oldest to go to dinner with them. Kevin and Kyle said, "Danny, please come, and then maybe Vicky will not come." But Eddie did it again; Vicky showed up. Kevin, on purpose, spilled his soda on her, and Danny left the table during dinner. Danny told me he was thankful he knew some old friends at the restaurant. Danny said they were oblivious to anything but themselves. Danny told me he was mad he was tricked—he thought it was going to be just the guys. He said he told Eddie just that fact when they got into the car to leave.

Danny said, "Mom, why did I bother to go?" Plus, Danny is still not happy with Eddie for the way he treated all of us—the nasty talking and the driveway episodes. Danny had gone out there many times and said, "Why are you acting this way?" Danny has strong values and was disgusted with Eddie at this point.

The boys even told Eddie, "We do not want Vicky coming with us." And of course Eddie's favorite saying was, "Too bad, get over it, you cannot tell me what to do. You will do what I say and go where I say." He was losing his children over this issue—they felt horrible. I could see that, in my opinion, Eddie was pushing this woman on them!

I remember Eddie saying to me, "No one will ever want you. You're crazy!" I think inside he must have had to prove he could "get" someone, anyone. I was not in a hurry; I was in shock, numb, and still grieving for my loss. My life was in turmoil—my divorce had not even begun to be settled. I filed; I wanted out of this madness!

Eventually, I did join a Christian online dating Web site. I met a chaplain in the military. His name was Jerry, and he was handsome and kind. We talked back and forth via e-mail. But with all that was going on, I really was not ready for any serious relationship. A man like Jerry could tell that was the case, I am sure, and I did not want to tell him my issues. In my heart, I wanted to be whole, but I was not whole and knew it. I was still a zombie reeling from my emotional battering.

Kevin and Kyle really acted up every time they came home from being with Eddie. All the children were telling me that Vicky was talking trash about me, right in front of them. I would send the insurance co-pays in an envelope with them so Eddie could pay half. That helped with food money for us. Emily had been sick and the co-pays were adding up.

One time, I sent the co-pays and the boys told me that Vicky picked them up from the table, looked at the envelope, threw the paperwork on the floor, and said, "What is this shit?" The children also came home and told me how much she made fun of me; and called me names. My God, this is their mom she is talking badly about! I cannot believe this! This woman does not even know me! What the heck is Eddie telling her, I wondered. My insides were panicked with terror.

I called Eddie on the phone and talked to him about the co-pay money. He would not pay the bills for many weeks, sometimes months. Then he would not pay what he owed— he would deduct things and say he already paid them. Confusing crap! Crazy-making! He was doing the same thing with the co-pays as he was doing with my life.

I would stress out so badly about those co-pays. Yes, I realized that this was about control and crazy-making. It made me sick and I would shake before I handed him the paperwork for the co-pays. My insides felt like I had a blender beating up my blood and guts under my skin; I had a crawling feeling inside my body.

I told him, "I need the money and it is tough on me and the children. I am getting help from my church and getting food from the food pantry."

He replied, "Work harder, Amy! It is your own fault you wanted the divorce, and you got it."

I went into shock; I started crying and hung up on him. How could he be so heartless and mean? That is what bullies do. Why? I would ask myself: why did I marry this man? My whole insides and my whole being were fried; I was numb. For the life of me I could not understand why he had the need to punish me and the children. This is all like mental torture. All I could do was wait till the next shock, the next vomit of his words.

One Saturday he took the boys for the day; they came

home and told me all about their day. I was glad they liked to tell me about their day, I felt better knowing that they were safe. Bobbie, from the shelter, said that was okay. I did not like hearing about the drunken parties and him swaying down the stairs from the neighbor's house. But at least I could monitor their safety. I missed them so much when they were gone. I had never really had them out of my sight since their birth.

They came home that day and told me something the made me sick to my stomach: they went for a boat ride on a lake with a man and Vicky's daughter, Sarah.

I asked, "Who was the man?"

Kevin said, "We did not know, maybe Sarah's grandfather."

I asked, "Where was your dad?"

Kevin said, "At the camp house with Vicky."

I asked, "You did have life jackets on, right?"

Both of them piped up and said, "No, we did not."

Now I am upset. Eddie sent them out on a boat with a stranger and no life jackets! I thought to myself, what if something had happened and the boat overturned? Who would have saved them? The man would have saved his granddaughter first! I wanted to cry. I lost a brother to drowning! There had been multiple accidents in the news lately, in which fathers have taken their boys fishing and the boat capsized. They have drowned and the reasons were: NO LIFE JACKETS! I was definitely in PTSD mode; I got angry and felt helpless. I was upset and felt that Eddie could not even keep them safe. Why did he not go out with them on the lake? I thought, that should not have happened when it comes to your children's lives.

I was now on guard! I was in panic mode! When he had

them, he needed to take care of them and be with them. I was not going to bury a child! I thought, what an ASS Eddie was! I thought to myself, nothing else seemed to matter to him but Vicky, and those kids knew it! I brought this incident up to Dr. Tim, and he talked to Eddie about my concern, and guess what? Eddie told Dr. Tim it was just a quick ride, no big deal, they were out there less than five minutes. I was angry; in my opinion, I could see that Eddie again justified his behavior—like it was…just a little wet T-shirt contest…no big deal. Whether it was five minutes or one hour, drowning takes just a few moments and it happens quickly—ask anyone who has that type of loss! I believe that every child should have a life jacket on when riding in a boat. I do not believe, in my heart, that I am overexaggerating, not at all!

This camp, a little lake house, was owned by Vicky's family. And this place was the beginning of Kevin's and Kyle's greater distance from their dad. Now they had less chance of ever being close to him. It all just kept piling up.

I called Bobbie at the Battered Women's Shelter, and she met with me. I was so frightened at the thought of him not paying attention to them—they would get hurt. Bobbie taught me to teach them about safety; basically, the boys needed to take care of each other and to keep each other safe. I told them to call me or their counselor, Dr. Tim, if they did not feel safe; just tell someone. They had his number with them at all times.

I remember that Eddie would not pay attention to them or to me when we were together; I was the one mostly responsible for the children. If I asked him to help, I was the bitch. I knew in my heart of hearts, I felt he could not keep them safe. They needed to learn to do that for themselves.

Imagine that: a drill for the boy's safety from the Battered Women's Shelter; who would have thought. Thank God for Bobbie for helping us through that. She has helped me through so much.

I remember a few months ago when I went out to dinner with a man, yes, a man. I needed to feel like a human being. I am a beautiful woman and I am sane. I needed to test that water. So I went out for a casual dinner with a man who was not my type. So that was safe, no attachments required. I had a few glasses of wine and came home. I had a right to go out; the children were with Eddie. Usually I go out with my best friend, Lynn, to the movies on those nights when he had them. But this night was different; I needed to do this dinner thing. I came home and we talked a little, then said good-night. I did the kiss- and-hug-thing, and off he went. I had my pajamas on and was at the computer checking my e-mail when all of a sudden, the kids came to the office and said, "Mom, the police are here and want to see you."

I jumped up out of the office chair and ran down the stairs. I thought, "Oh, my God!" Someone in my family must be hurt or dead." I got to the kitchen, scared to death to hear what they were going to say to me.

I went into the kitchen and there were two officers. I looked at them and said, "What has happened? Who is hurt?" But what they did say was unbelievable. The officers explained to me that they had received a call from my soon-to-be-ex-husband asking them to check on the welfare of his children. He reported that I was falling down drunk and with a strange man, and that one of the children had called him and the youth pastor.

I said, "Really? Do I look like I am falling down drunk? I am in my pajamas, reading my e-mail, and going to bed soon. I did go out to dinner with a man friend and had couple glasses of wine, and was laughing."

The officers said, "By law, we have to investigate a welfare call to make sure you are okay and that the children are okay, and your ex-husband is nearby to take custody of the children, just in case."

I said, "Oh, really, where is he?"

"Down the street," said one of the officers. The officers were very nice. They said, "Sorry we bothered you, we can see you are fine." Then they looked at the children and said, "Your mom is allowed to have some drink if she wants, and to go out." The officers left, and my head was foggy. What the heck? I go to dinner and the police are called. My children had never seen me with any man other than their father.

In the report filed there was this comment: "The officer concluded that Amy Howard was not intoxicated...no cause for complaint was found regarding the welfare of all persons at the house!" I thought, oh, Eddie tried to take advantage of getting something incriminating on me. I needed to be careful about what I did. Can I breathe without being crucified? I am on guard; I am ready for him to try to get me.

I am amazed. Eddie has been seen sitting at the bar, drinking like a fish, with the children downstairs; taking the children to full-blown parties; and seeing other women right along. Does he feel he has a right to go out to dinner, drag them with him, then leave them alone for hours? Then I go out ONCE and almost get my children taken away—for what?

Because he thinks I am falling down drunk! I thought to

myself, he HOPED I was falling down drunk; he wanted to take the children from me. He was trying to do what he said he would. It is said that "Thou that cast the first stone…"

I have not followed him around; I want him to leave me alone. He will stop at nothing to see me suffer, to make me look like a crazy drunk, and a two-timing lunatic! I was feeling paranoid at the way Eddie would always find things out about me—any little thing I said or did—you'd think I'd committed the crime of the century! He twisted EVERY-THING! Was I being followed? Who is talking to him? Who can I trust? Oh, God, please make this nightmare STOP!

I talked to Bobbie about this; I felt bad for even going out on a date. I really did not want to go out, but Bobbie said, "This is normal that you did go—most women do; they want to see another side of normal dating, compared to the hell of being with this type of an abuser." So—I was okay. And yes, he did what abusers do: accuse the victim of what they are doing themselves, and take away all that they can from the victim. This whole thing was cruel; I am a good mom. He cannot ever take that away from me, ever.

Things just seemed to be getting worse for the children; he again picked them up for the midweek dinner. When the boys returned home, they said we went to his apartment and watched a movie. I said, "Oh, that's nice." I usually stayed quiet as long as I knew they had stayed safe. During the week, or just all of a sudden, they would say something to me that was bothering them.

Kyle had one of those moments. He looked at me so sadly and said, "Mom, I went to the bathroom at Dad's apartment while the movie was on, and I walked by his computer. There was a screen-saver picture of Dad and Vicky with Winnie the Pooh at Disneyland. Dad went to Disney with Vicky and has never taken me."

I saw the hurt on that boy's face. He said, "I never want to go to Disney, Mom! Can you someday take me to Universal Studios?" I told Kyle, "When I have the money I would be happy to take you."

I was heartbroken for my children. Eddie takes trips to Florida all the time now that he has left us. He drives his dad's car down there for him in the winter, and in the spring he brings it back for him. I remember when he had first left I begged him to take Danny he had just graduated from high school, and it would have been a good road trip. Eddie said no; he was driving straight through and back. No time to do anything special.

I think now he really wanted to stop off in New Jersey to see a certain woman he had met at the onsite rehab. Danny would have been in his way. He had also taken my one family member's husband who thinks I am everything Eddie says I am—crazy, that is. And he's taken Vicky, and God knows who else. But never once did he make that trip with his own children, never.

He brought them back pins for their jackets and a sweatshirt for Emily, which she has never worn. They were disgusted! Kyle and Kevin do not look at Winnie the Pooh the same way anymore; neither does Emily.

It just seemed like it could get no worse for the loss of a family and the loss of a father who never was really there for them. He was never really my husband either, except maybe in a false reality that I built in my own mind. I have never known anyone like this—one who wants self-gratification at all costs. Even human life did not matter to him for even his own needs; here we were living inside a fake scene of a "happy marriage"—inside four walls of complete secrecy. There were far too many hurts he was putting the children through—he was actually driving them away from him.

There was an example of a real whopper of an eye-opener, one that the boys will never forget, nor will I, nor Emily. Every time Eddie took them for the weekend I gave them big hugs and off they went. I always would say, "Have a good time and stay safe."

Emily and I went to dinner at Kay and John's house. They had moved back here, not one mile from us. So it was wonderful. Kay had a nice get-together at her house with friends and family. After dinner my cell phone rang. It was Kyle, wanting to come home.

I asked him, "Did you tell your dad you wanted to come home?" I could hear the tears and quietness in my son.

Kyle said, "No, Mom; I am afraid to tell him. Will you tell him?"

We had talked about this. If they were ever in an uncomfortable situation they could tell Eddie or call Dr. Tim, or me. I knew if Kyle had to sneak away and make a phone call, it was not good. I told Kyle, "Put your dad on the phone and I will tell him." I was scared myself to have to talk to Eddie; I wanted to cry, knowing my son was uncomfortable. I did not know where he was or whom he was with. This felt so out of control for me. How was I to protect Kyle and Kevin?

Eddie gets on the phone and I say, "Kyle wants to come home and he is afraid to tell you." Quickly, Eddie says, "They are more afraid of you than me!"

I could not believe what I had just heard; my hand started to shake—the receiver on the phone was shaking uncontrollably. I started to cry; I could not believe he had just said that to me and about me! He said it loud enough so that wherever he was, anyone near him could hear what he had said. No one could hear what I was saying—just Emily and Kay. I hung up with shock and tears. My children are not afraid of me! It was him we were all afraid of! So, whoever was there, it was his show, it was what he was mirroring of himself. He was making me out to be this horrible person.

I called Dr. Tim and left a message—Kyle and Kevin were somewhere and they were uncomfortable. I tried to call the boys back, but Eddie had shut the phone off. Emily called him and left him a message; she was mad that her dad was not listening to her brothers. She fights with them at times, but she loves them very much. She wanted them to come home if they were not happy. He never called back. I went through a whole night of not knowing what was wrong with Kyle. Why he was uncomfortable? Why did he want to come home?

I ran out to the front yard at Kay's house, I did not want to look like I was overreacting, as Eddie would always say about me. But I really did not want everyone to see me cry. This is not normal! People do not live like this! Do they? If I have this type of trauma about my children, what about the ones who are beaten and neglected? I love my children so much; I do not want them hurt, either mentally or physically! But Eddie and Vicky were hurting them! Why? I just wanted out of a bad marriage; he was not going to change…Oh, God, help me!

I did not sleep that night. I went to church the next day; he did not bring them to Sunday school. We had agreed that they attend Sunday school. I had to wait until six o'clock to find out if Kevin and Kyle were okay. Eddie dropped them off at the evening Bible study.

When Kevin and Kyle arrived, they looked like they had not slept all weekend. And they both poured out what happened all weekend. They never wanted to go back with their dad, ever!

They had to sleep in the same room with Sarah and her friend. That is yucky for boys to sleep in the same room with little girls! Especially ones they really did not know, and the girls were much younger than they were. I thought, how inappropriate.

Kevin was a mess. He said, "I heard them through the walls of this little camp. I heard them having sex, Mom. I know that is what it was. It was banging and banging on the wall. Over and over again!" Kevin said.

Kyle said, "Mom, I just sat there at the edge of the bed; I wanted to come home. I waited for the noise to stop. I felt alone and I wanted to come home."

Kevin was mad; Kyle was sad. Kevin had a different atti- tude—he was grossed out about this. Kevin was angry; his dad had lied to him.

He said, "Mom, Dad said he was going to sleep on the couch. But he was not there when I needed him in the night. Then, when I got up in the morning, Vicky had no clothes on. She just had a sheet on and they were both on the front porch."

What could I say? I was horrified to see their condition of disarray. The boys have been exposed to so much with Eddie; how much more can these children take? I really did not care anymore about him; it was the children I cared for, and my fear of what was yet to come. I feel he hates me with all his being and so does Vicky!

But I could not get out of my mind Eddie telling me that the boys were more afraid of me, than him. Lies and more Lies!

CHAPTER 9
A DISTORTED MIND

I was in such a panic mode, not only for me but for my children. My mind was on overtime; I felt so sick to my stomach. It was my mind that truly concerned me; I was on guard to what Eddie was going to do and say to me next, but now I was on guard for the children's sakes and safety. I felt like a mother bear guarding her cubs.

Was I feeling normal fear or was it irrational fear? This is where I really questioned myself. Was it the sane me, the me I know that is in there; beyond the madness? Has something in my mind been distorted? Or was I feeling the PTSD symptoms, double-barreled, right between my eyes? No one understood me, I needed help.

All this with Eddie was not normal! I struggled to maintain my sanity for my children. I was going to fight the good fight, with my faith! That was and is my strength, for without that faith I would fail.

The divorce proceedings were going slowly. Eddie really thought he could have everything; it was all about the money. Sad, that after all the many years of marriage it has to come down to the money—not about the family. What was good for the children, in my opinion, was not good for Eddie.

I went to the courthouse with my lawyer a few times, trying to settle, but Eddie wanted more and more. It cost me more and more each time. He now earned double my income. His lawyer was helping the "poor fireman" who was getting taken to the cleaners—Eddie even told me that. According to Eddie's first financial statement, his lawyer charged him NOTHING, and I was up around $9,000 and climbing up to $11,000.

So, yes, he could keep coming back at me. I was teetering on financial ruin and scared almost to the point of zombie-hood, like in movies where the zombies walk around in trances, in groups. They know where they are going but they just stare out into space. I felt that way 24/7; the stress of what Eddie is doing to the children and me has me in total shock. In a way, I always knew he would never let me just leave and divorce nicely. I know now that fear always kept me there with him.

I had so many questions and thoughts: Eddie either wanted the house sold in order to get his share of the money, or he wanted for me to buy him out. I could not buy him out; the cost of the Victorian home would have been too much for me to handle. I agreed to sell; Eddie had refinanced the home a few times, so there was no equity to split. I told my lawyer to give him everything but the children: one-third of the business, my vehicle, and the furniture. I needed to live and provide for myself and the children. My lawyer knew Eddie was not going to stop trying to get it all from me; I was a wreck.

In my opinion, Eddie acted ridiculously when we went to court to try one more time to settle. Our lawyers had threatened to quit, due to him wanting nuts, bolts, cords, and other stupid things at the twelfth hour of settling. I could not believe this guy; he got everything he wanted: the 401k, his state retirement (of which I have none), the minivan (paid for), the antique car (paid for), the time share, cemetery plots, his two-thirds of our business, and yet he also wanted the leather recliner. Eddie had even cleared out more things in the garage the day before the divorce proceedings. My lawyer had had enough! So had his! They were both going to quit; I just wanted to be as far away from Eddie as I could! I could not even breathe; I would shake to be anywhere near him. My fear was so great!

He hated the fact that I got anything. I did get to keep my car. I had bought a Mercedes SUV. I still had payments, which I made with my bonus money every month. After my accident I wanted a tank! I wanted something I would feel safe to drive, something that had the steel cage roll bar. The price was right—same as a Chrysler top-of-the-line minivan. I loved cars, remember? So I shopped for safety and reliability.

Eddie told me that he told people, "Look, she is the snob with the Mercedes, and look at me—I ride around with a crappy minivan." Yes what a poor fireman, he is being taken to the cleaners. But I worked for my safety. I believe he was really jealous! As he said, "He wanted me with no car, no house, no children, and no nothing." I was surprised he did not go after the kids, but I did get physical custody of the children. At this point I felt he was more concerned about "his money."

He also lied to the judge; he told her he was going to be just a fireman, that he did not want to work two jobs, and that he wanted to spend more time with his three growing children. She granted him that no man should have to work over forty hours. He was selling his business, but I did surprise him with the $30,000 receipts that day. He really does believe I am an idiot. I did get my third of that; I really fought for that; it made up for the child support I was not going to get, since he was only going to make a fireman's wage. But my lawyer and I knew better—he always worked more than one job, even before we married. He lied!

As I stood next to my lawyer, for whom I have deep feelings, as he became a good friend and tried so hard to help me and the children, I felt proud he always did the right thing to not put me through to much crap. He knew what kind of person Eddie was, and to have me as a client he had to have the patience of Job. But I will never forget that day, standing in front of that judge, scared to death. I was very shaken up by Eddie's whole immature demeanor.

The judge looked at the agreement and looked right at me and said, "Is this going to be enough?" She was concerned!

I started to cry and grabbed my lawyer's arm. I knew I'd given Eddie too much; it made me sick. I was sick about the lack of child support. It was not the children's fault; it was about "his money." I wanted this divorce over and so did these two lawyers. I was shaken up very much at this outcome. I had no choice—I needed to do what was right for my welfare and for the children's. I felt as if I was victimized by Eddie also, with this outcome, not only by the abuse in his actions outside the court, but legally also. I lost all respect for our state rep for supporting this insanity.

I looked at her, crying, and said, "It will have to do."

So be it! Happy Holidays to me! My home was sold, the children were devastated. They were like pack rats; they grew up in this home. Poor Emily could not sleep over at other people's homes due to her allergies, fear, and discomfort of not being in her own room. This was truly a children's home—it was big with lots of room to have fun. I always had a houseful of children. They were definitely going to miss this home.

Where to begin? I had to find a place to live and the means of getting sufficient finances. I was blessed to have good business friends. First, I called the mortgage company who had done all the refinancing for Eddie, and I and told him the situation. He did some financial magic and got me qualified for a loan. I had always had good credit, but this loan was magic and a miracle!

My old neighbor from the other side of town was a real estate agent. I called and asked her to look around for something in my price range. We went looking; the kids and I walked into one place and saw mold all over the walls and ceiling. The roof had a leak and the structure looked nasty. The children ran out of there choking; their allergies got the best of them with the mold. We finally found a place just right for us; it was small and a little more money, but we could make it a home. I would work hard for them. Another miracle and another prayer answered. "Thank you, God!"

My thoughts were with Eddie and what he had said: "I really do not care where you live; you deserve to live in an apartment." With that statement, I thought he did not care where his children were moving—unbelievable! Before we moved in, Eddie came to pick up the boys at the new house; we were there, cleaning.

I asked Eddie, "Do you want to see the inside so you know where your children will be sleeping and living?"

He replied, "No, I have already been inside. I was there when they did the smoke test through the fire department."

Oh, my God, I went into shock and wanted to puke! I felt like he had violated me and my new home. He already has seen the floor plan and the inside! How sick is that? I wondered if he had done anything inside, or was he just getting madder and jealous that I have achieved and taken care of the children. No, he would not understand that this was about the children; he seemed to look at it like I had everything. In a way, I have the love and respect of my children and that, to me, would be everything.

I had also refinanced my car so I could afford the payments, and I was moving along really well, trying to transition into single motherhood. But things were really bad the day we moved from the Victorian. All the church men showed up to move us—there was so much to move and pack. Ten years worth and three floors of household stuff, moving into a small, cape-style home. I felt so out of sorts; the men were just filling up the moving truck as fast as they could. I realized I did not have the heart, nor could I pack up my bedroom. It was such a feeling of loss. I started to cry, and Jim, one of the men from church, came over and just gave me a hug. Then all the others came to me and started to pray, as I felt my feet slip out from under me. I felt so weak, but I did not fall. Those men held me up with hugs and prayers. It was a moment that only God could have had his hand in. The loss and grieving for my home and my life as I knew it slipped away, just as the children were looking at me to be their strength. It was an incredible moment. I had to pull myself together; lots of people came to help us.

At church the next day it was mentioned that in all the years of men moving and helping people, they had never seen so many people come to a move as there were that day.

So here we were in our new little home; it is cute and the children were comfy with it. We were walking on all the faith we had. Many miracles were part of getting us where we were and we all knew it. We found unexpected food store gift cards signed by Jesus on our back porch, unexpected money in Christmas cards signed with love, and well wishes for Christmas presents for the children. I know what having love from a church family felt like. We had a Charlie Brown tree that year, but it was the best Christmas ever—we had a home, we had food, and we had each other.

The children had not been wanting to go with Eddie; I would be at work when he came to get them, and they would refuse to go out and get into the car. So then, the nightmare began again! I could not make them go when I was at work, and when I was home I would leave the room when I knew he was coming or calling, and let them handle him themselves.

At this point in my life, I cannot have contact with Eddie; his verbal abuse is out of control and his hatred and vengeance toward me is incredible. My whole being would shake if he was near me, and he would trigger my Post Traumatic Stress; he traumatized me every time. He was also traumatizing the children, although he could not see it. He would blame everything on me. If they acted up he would say, "They never acted like that when I was home." Like I changed them! He was never home to really see how they acted. But if they acted up he insisted that I must be doing something to them.

Well, the time was coming for the nightmare to start again; I could feel it. I was on guard and ready! I was right; the sheriff came and served me papers. Eddie was charging me with contempt for alienation of the children. I was horrified that he would do this to me. I had no money to defend myself! Here we go again! Panic, fear, and shock set in. I was not going to lose my children; I am a good person and a good mother!

Emily was talking to her dad; he and Vicky planned on trying to get custody; they said they were more stable than I was! They even refinanced Vicky's condo to make new bedrooms in the basement and bought a boat for the lake house, and YES, he was still working his two jobs, going to Florida, eating out, and living life like a king; and he called me a Queenie, imagine that! And it was all about me!

I was struggling to maintain a home, doing all the motherly duties and working fifty hours a week. The children are good children; they are in a stable home. What, is he crazy? Emily said that Vicky gets drunk all the time, and they both talk badly about me in front of her. Emily tried to stay with them for a while; as a fifteen-year-old, she did not like Mom's rules. She thought the rules would be better with her dad, but there were none. So she learned some life lessons and came back home to us in the little cape house. She told me stories of her dad and Vicky getting so drunk, she had to help her dad home from the beach to the camp one night. I thought to myself, who is not stable? Imagine that: a fifteen-year-old has to help her drunken dad home. Also, the same night, a twenty-year-old boy was hitting on my daughter while her dad and girlfriend were so very drunk!

Emily also told me that I was never to talk to Betsey, my friend from the auto parts call center, again. I said, "Why?" Emily said, "Betsey knows Vicky, they are old friends." I could not believe what I was hearing: why are there so many people wanting to see me fail? I just could not believe Betsey would know Vicky. I had to think long and hard, and I did see some things in court get twisted about me. Betsey knew I was dating a chaplain whom I'd met online. Eddie said to the lawyers in court at the alienation hearing that I was dating men online from out of state! Trying to make me look nasty and whoreish! My lawyer said I have a right to date whomever I wanted!

It would have been something for me to ask Jerry to come to New England and testify for me, in his full uniform. He is one of the top military chaplains for the U.S. military. He designed the code of ethics for our country! I was with a very honorable man and I was not ashamed of that at all. I wished we could have worked out; he made my heart flutter like a teenager, but the timing was off—maybe the chemistry, also. I never told him about my Post Traumatic Stress; I wanted him to see me for me. He was a breath of fresh air; I did meet him after many months of dating online, and we have stayed friends. I would have moved to get away from Eddie and Vicky; I think she is just as spiteful as he is. Now my opinion is that their relationship is a match made in hell.

So! Every casual conversation with Betsey went right to Vicky. Heck, I was doing nothing wrong, so what did they have on me—ZIP. But it was the twisting, the crazy-making, and the fear they put in me about losing the children that was horrendous. For example, when I was married to him, he would take a small incident and blow it up into something really big. He messed with my mind, and my soul. Also, I wondered how much *did* Betsy hurt me in my divorce? This is all so sick; imagine intentionally hurting a wounded person!

I thank God for my friend and mentor, Gracie, from church. She went to every court hearing with me. I could not bear to sit there by myself and listen to my name and character be slandered. Eddie even brought his family to court with him, and Vicky, too. They all reminded me of the hecklers on *The Muppets*—idiots, in a way. I wish they knew my heart, I wished they really knew me. But they all were twisting things; if I was a monster, then my mind was truly distorted. Was I just imagining that I was good? Gracie was there to make my reality real for me. Just as in abuse cases, the abuser distorts reality. Eddie was doing it so well; he had so many people believing him. I had God, and he is bigger than that boogeyman across the courtroom. I was scared and frightened of him, yes, but as Gracie would say, "Good always overcomes evil." She would not get involved, but she would pray for me and be a great sister.

Eddie was also going on and on to my lawyer at the courthouse about me having an online blog site. I thought, right—that is for kids; Emily has an account but I do not. I would be embarrassed to have a journal online. Why would I? Why would he think I had one? And why would he bring this up at the courthouse? I hope they did not create one for me! Anything to make me look bad, or was it my "on guard" mode?

At night, weird things started to happen to my car when I moved into our new home; my car was getting egged about ten-thirty every Friday night. I got paintballed, also. I thought to myself, maybe I cannot have a Mercedes in a middle-income neighborhood, or, maybe the kids here hate my Benz. After a while I started to call and report the incidences to the police every time.

My job at the dealership was getting strained; I thought maybe I would find a corporate job, like when I worked for BOSE. I wanted to find work where I could use my mind, and dig my feet in, and be happy.

A communications company hired me in a business development position; I loved it! I was meeting people and enjoying my work. My boss, Pat, was awesome. She worked with me, but she could see the pain and torment I was experiencing due to Eddie. She was afraid for my life. As verbally abusive as he was, some people thought he might turn dangerous. Pat did worry about me. She heard some of the phone calls and saw me running outside crying because of something horrible he said.

One time, I was on a business trip out of town with my group. Eddie called about five times, leaving messages for me. The boys would not get in the car with him, and he was yelling at me on the cell phone. He said, "Who is the parent here?" I wanted to laugh at him! If he was a parent he would have a relationship with them, and they would want to go on their visits. I could not help him; I was out of town.

The children hated to see me when I had the court dates. I was a mess; I could not believe he was really doing this. I asked myself many questions, like what is wrong with this man?

Then things started to sink: the court dates were increasing, my credit card was maxed in lawyer's fees, defending myself. Try $15,000 in lawyer's fees over the course of two years!

Emily was always sick. The children were always sick; I had to take time off to take them to the doctor because Eddie would not help. My boss was getting upset I was taking so much time off. The company felt bad, but between the court dates and doctors, I had to find something more flexible. Things were not feeling right. I was on guard and I could not sleep. I was getting phone calls about midnight or so; people were laughing and partying and I would hang up. I was anxious about my surroundings. I wished it all would end.

I had to take the children to the court counselor; it was a court order. They wanted to talk to the children alone. The court would then get their answer and decide what was going to happen. I prayed to God, "Please let my children have a voice." I knew in my heart of hearts I had done nothing wrong, but what scared the hell out of me was Eddie and his persistence to try and get what he wanted. He just did not stop twisting and twisting things in his favor. Is that not a scary mental thing?

The court decided that there was no alienation and it was dismissed. Eddie was fuming mad! He snapped at my lawyer. He hated not getting his way; his true colors showed that. The really sick thing is that he really believes I had alienated his children from him. The louder one speaks; one should look in the mirror, because that finger is pointing right back at you.

The judge also told Eddie he needed to get some counseling with the children because they were growing up, and he might lose all hope of a positive relationship with them. We set things up so he could do that with Dr. Tim. I also tried to file for court fees because I had not alienated his children, and my attorney's fees were too unbelievably high for me to handle. In my opinion, the judge did not like women; she denied my restitution. I wanted to cry and throw up at the same time. How was I ever going to pay these legal debts off?

Dr. Tim had a plan: he wanted to concentrate on getting Kevin and Eddie on track. With all Kevin had seen, and the way Kevin was with Eddie, Eddie just did not understand him. Kevin was a great kid, very smart and sensitive. Things could not get any worse. Eddie had the boys for band night for the school football game; he was to watch them play and bring them home. Well, Eddie and Kyle wanted to stay and hang out with their friends. But Kevin was tired and cold and wanted to come home; this was early November and they had marched all day with the band. Kevin ended up throwing a cup of hot chocolate at Eddie. Eddie brought them home and came to the door, and he proceeded to tell me how bad Kevin had been.

I was standing there thinking how I needed to try and help Eddie understand why Kevin was tired. I was being nice in front of the boys. Eddie just needed to figure out how to build a relationship with his sons.

So I told Eddie, "You just have to have patience with him, have some understanding, and listen to both of them when they are talking."

Well, Eddie was not going to listen to me, since "I am an idiot," and they were not going to tell him what to do, let alone my standing there trying to reason with him. He went off on a horrible verbal assault on me right in front of the boys. The things he said were madness! Nothing made sense. In a matter of moments, he brought up every sin I had ever committed, even ones I had forgotten all about. How could someone remember someone's sins like that—he twisted and blew up everything he could think of! This was the worse assault of them all! I was shaking terribly. I stood across the kitchen thinking, "Okay, Bobbie, what do I do in this situation?" Do not feed his fit of tantrum! Do not cry! Take control, set the boundary! That's it—set the boundary!

I said, "Get out of my house!" I was shaking uncontrollably, just like a child who had done nothing wrong to deserve this type of punishment! I was keeping it together, not arguing with him, not crying. I just kept saying, "Get out of my house!"

Eddie just would not stop; I went into a disassociated state of mind. I just wanted him to go! I leaned over to the table and grabbed my purse, thinking how I would like to throw this right at him, but I knew better. But I hung onto it like a security blanket, and it was shaking with me. I had a hold of it so hard, trembling and shaking. Then Eddie looked at me and said, "Just look at yourself, you are crazy."

I lost it; I threw the purse at the chair in front of him and screamed, "Get out of my house NOW!" He left, all right, but he was still flapping his mouth as he was walking out and down the sidewalk to his car. I felt so bad for the boys; they just stood in the kitchen, in shock at this display of verbal torture. We all looked at each other in a zombie stare; we could not believe what just had happened.

I told the boys this was just wrong—men are not supposed to act this way. Then, there was a knock on the door and it was the police. I had forgotten that I had called them to report another assault on my car. Pink paintballs! Too bad the officer had not come five minutes before, and then we would have been saved from the verbal domestic vomit of Eddie. They had just missed him. I got paintballed again tonight! It is either eggs or paintballs. When it happens, I can hear people yelling outside, then Boom! I jump out of my skin. This has to stop. I have done nothing to anyone, and neither have my children. Someone hates my car!

I am shaken, but not broken. My mind is wounded, but not dead. I pray for peace. I am stable and grounded. My mind is not distorted from what the reality of truth is. I thank God for a sound mind everyday.

A distorted mind is an unstable mind…

CHAPTER 10
SURVIVAL & THE STALKER

I thought to myself, "Why?" Why did Eddie have to do an all-out verbal attack on me in front of Kevin and Kyle? Both boys could not believe he had done that and said all the crazy things he said. How sad; I was trying to do what the court said. For me, to even try and reason with him was showing I was trying to help him "make nice," trying to help him understand them. I don't think he'll ever have a relationship with them like this—the boys see their dad as a mean man. I did not deserve any of that. No one deserves to be treated that way. I felt breathless and numb.

What makes someone snap like that? I hear those words, "Let him have his tantrum and then he will stop." I saw that during my whole marriage; I could never understand why, never. The boys do not want to be like that when they grow up, that's for sure. I thought, how sad that Eddie cannot see that his children cannot even respect him. He scared them, as he does me! With all that anger, I think he would kill me if he could do it and get away with it. This is very distorted! I vowed that night that Eddie was on his own to "make nice" with his children. I will never take that type of treatment again.

I was not sleeping well at night; I would wake with dreams, and I could hear every noise in and around the house. I did not feel safe. My property was getting bombed weekly! Eggs was the first weapon of choice, and now paintballs. My car was the target; I was getting tired of it! I really started calling the police every time now to report the vandalisms, so I would have it documented in case we could catch whoever was doing this.

The police asked me, "Do you know who would do this to you?"

I thought, maybe the kids, my ex-husband, maybe, but I said, "But I do not believe he would stoop to that level."

The police beefed up the patrol around my house. I even sat in my car one night; I wanted to catch them. I know it was more than one person, because of all the noise they made screaming and laughing. The screaming sounded violent, like yelling with meanness, but when they ran away they were laughing.

I was having trouble with the Benz; I had just replaced the front ball joints and now the back suspension needed work. I could have fixed it; my car payments were under $250 a month, but I was sick and tired of the bombings. So I decided to trade in my car. I bought a cute Tiger Woods Buick SUV, fully loaded, with a lot of the same features as the Benz. I will miss my other car, but I figured this was for the best. Whoever was jealous would stop bothering my car and my family now.

I was wrong! Now my house started getting bombed with eggs. The first time we heard bangs of noise and went outside, someone had bombed Emily's bedroom window, which was the master bedroom upstairs. Also, in the back door to the mudroom, eggs got in between the screen and all over the sidewalk on the garage, high up.

Either they were mad at Emily or they thought that was my bedroom. I asked Emily, "Who could be doing this?"

She said, "Mom, I have no idea!" Emily is a good kid. She has a tight group of friends she has grown up with. She is good; she does not hang around with the wrong crowds.

I had to borrow Kay's husband's power washer to clean the eggs off. Unfortunately, the eggers must have let the eggs rot, and my home has permanent stains now. I even called my contractor; he said it would be $2,000 to replace the siding that is damaged. This is sickening, this is vandalism! This is criminal! There is also a hole in my siding near my garage where something hard hit it—not sure what it was that made the hole.

The next time, we were sitting there watching TV, and all of a sudden, there were the sounds of gun fire, Boom! You would swear the glass was broken on all the front windows; they came right up close to the windows. We could hear people yelling, laughing, and running. We would run outside every time, but the car would speed off before we got there. It scared the hell out of all of us; the kids even got to the point of calling them "the eggers." The boys would say, "Mom, do you think "the eggers" will come tonight?"

Now they were on guard! It felt like they were casing my home, hovering near the windows. Were they looking at us, first? This is all so ill.

This vandalism was like something out of a nightmare! Here I have Post Traumatic Stress and someone was making it worse for me. Between what was wrong with me, Eddie, and court, I was on the edge! Always waiting for what was next! My skin was crawling!

Eddie is still trying to "make nice" in his own way, but the children don't trust him. He took them one night for their normal nightly dinner. I went out on my weekly dinner date with my girlfriends to Friendly's. We sat around, laughed, and talked about those Red Sox, and just enjoyed the moment. I was there that evening with Kay and Gracie, when my cell phone rang. It was Eddie—he had a panic in his voice. I thought one of the children was hurt, but instead he said, "Kevin has been acting up all night."

I said, "Why are you calling me?" I did not want to hear about it, not after the last go-round on band night. No Way! I said, "Eddie, you have to deal with him yourself. I cannot get involved anymore."

Eddie then said, "My fist accidentally touched Kevin's mouth. The kid trashed my car. I went into the house where I live because I needed to go grab my checkbook, and when I came out the car was trashed. I grabbed him and took him out of the car and my fist hit his lip by accident. I am bringing him home now."

Here I am sitting at dinner with my best friends and they hear what Eddie is saying, and we are all thinking— yeah, right! Eddie is guilty, I can hear it in his voice, and he is scared. Why? I thought Eddie was not scared of anything.

I told my friends I had better go home; I asked Kay to come with me. Gracie went home; I told her I would call her later. Kay came to my house, and we waited. Then Kevin burst though the door, madder than a wet hen. Blood was on his coat, and he was holding a tissue to his mouth. I thought to myself, Eddie has really lost it now.

Kevin said, "He punched me, that guy punched me with his fist. Mom, I want to go to the police station now! I want to file assault charges on him."

I said, "Okay, slow down, buddy, tell me what happened."

Kevin began to tell me his side of the story. He said, "We had to go to Vicky's and I did not want to go, but Dad had to get his checkbook. Dad was inside Vicky's for quite awhile, and while he was in there I put some papers on his seat, so when he got in the car he would sit on them." I thought, okay, boys will be boys, and they were bored from waiting for him to come back out.

Kevin said, "Mom, when Dad got back to the car and saw the paper on his seat, he grabbed me and took me outside of the car and pushed me up against the car and punched me right on my mouth."

I felt so bad for the boys. We stopped the bleeding; his lip was swollen and he looked like he had been in a little fight.

Kyle said, "Oh, Mom, I have a check for you from Dad."

I looked at the check and it was for the full amount that was owed for the co-pays! He never pays what he owes! "He must be guilty!" I thought; this was out of his character to pay the co-pays, and in a way I felt sorry for him. He just does not get it. He is torturing all of us. This has to stop!

Thank God Kay was here with me. I wanted to take Kevin to the police station, but, knowing Eddie, he would make me look like the troublemaker and the vengeful ex-wife. This was my chance to file charges back on him for assaulting a minor. That would really be bad for his record, being a fireman and all. I felt sick at the thought of having to do that. I thought I would wait till morning and call my lawyer for the children's sake. As vengeful as Eddie is, I am not; I really felt sorry for him.

Kay agreed, "Amy, you are the better person; if the tables were turned, you would be in jail now."

I was afraid to make any moves without my lawyer; I felt that Eddie had made me numb and frozen like a stone. What could be next? I was waiting constantly and wondering what was he going to do next, to me and to the children.

Morning came; I was going to wait until nine o'clock, when my lawyer's office opened.

Kevin's lip was still swollen. I said to him, "Buddy, you have to go to school till I figure out what to do." School started at seven-thirty, and he had to go.

Kevin said, "Okay, Mom. Call me when you know what I can do." Then he said, "Mom, I have band this morning, and I cannot play my instrument with this swollen lip."

I thought, "He is right—he cannot play like that." So I wrote a note to the school: it said:

"Please excuse Kevin from playing band today, due to a swollen lip.

Sincerely, Amy Howard"

I felt so sick bringing Kevin to school. I wanted to call Eddie to tell him to come and talk to his child and make this right. I wanted to protect Eddie, and I knew I could not.

Never again will he hurt these kids, emotionally or physically, ever. I dropped Kevin and Kyle off at school and hoped and prayed for the best.

The school guidance counselor called me and told me she had called the Department of Social Services and reported child abuse. I should be expecting a call from the DSS. She has also already informed Eddie. She said, "He knew." I thought he did know something was coming, but better from the school and not from me.

I did tell Kevin that the lawyer would take care of everything and that the Department of Social Services would investigate. Kevin never wanted to be with his dad again. I could not, in my heart, have Kevin file assault charges against his dad. I thought, years down the road that would be hard for any relationship to heal. They both might be in a different place, in their maturity. I could always hope for change and healing; I am not vengeful and full of bitterness.

I went to court and got a temporary order, stating that Kevin did not have to be forced to go with Eddie. I was always afraid of Eddie—over and over again he would threaten me constantly with contempt of court if they did not go. I hated court; it was like a nightmare to think "court equals Eddie" after all he did to manipulate the court system during our divorce and alienation charges; anything with court and Eddie has me full of fear. And LOTS more money—he was also on his second lawyer, so go figure! None of the children were going to be forced to go; maybe he would wake up and be a dad to them.

Eddie and Kevin had a scheduled appointment for counseling with Dr. Tim; Eddie was supposed to pick him up. Kevin said, "No way am I getting in that car with him!"

This appointment was for the two of them to work out their issues. Well, Eddie had really blown it! I called Dr. Tim's office and left a message that I could not bring Kevin in because he was not riding with Eddie to meet him. I was at a Christian conference in Boston. I had paid for a writer's workshop with author Carol Kent, and I was not going to miss that for anything. So I cancelled Kevin's share of the appointment, but said it would be up to Eddie to attend his share of the appointment due to the circumstances. I did not want to get involved; I thought it would be best for Eddie to go and explain why Kevin did not want to go, and that he would be investigated by the DSS for the assault on Kevin.

To this day, I am not sure Eddie ever did tell Dr. Tim about the assault, but Dr. Tim sent both Eddie and I a letter of resignation. He did not want to be involved with our family; he sees no end in sight to help mend the difficulties facing our family, especially with Kevin refusing to go today. I wonder if Dr. Tim knew the whole story.

Eddie, being Eddie, would not even pay for the cancelled appointment; he harassed me for the payment! Can you believe it? He hit our son, and the poor kid is afraid of being with him again, and Eddie could not even go to see Dr. Tim by himself. Now I have to pay the co-pay, plus the missed appointment. How distorted is that?

During this time of waiting for the DSS to investigate, I came home and got an anonymous letter in the mail. The postmark was from out of town—the same town Vicky worked in—by chance, Emily knew that. The letter was typed and it was making fun of my religious belief—telling me I am not a good person; that I broke up my own family; that I am a two-timer; and that I hurt my children and

myself. It stated that I am spiteful and vindictive; I am miserable and unhappy; and that my children will turn against me
one day. The letter also told me to go back to church and find
someone else to make me happy. I am to change my ways,
and go back to church again. There were lots of exclamation
marks in the letter, like whoever wrote it was very angry.

I had to laugh at first; I am none of the above, and I go
to church every Sunday and to Bible studies during the week,
and I have had so much faith that I have even been able to
get through this hell of a divorce. My children love me; I
never slept around on Eddie, ever. But I know whoever wrote
this letter is someone from Eddie's camp of hecklers.

But then I started to think about the letter. Who would
be this sick to write me a letter like this? My heart started to
race—I just could not have peace while being married to
him. I divorced him—I had no choice; I was dying while
being married to him. He was a mistake—not my type; I
was charmed and deceived by him.

I have always been a Christian. Why would this letter-
writer think otherwise—because I was not being controlled
any more? That's it! This person did not know me; this person
did not live behind my four walls. I was not vindictive—I was
hurt and hurt badly, at that. My mind could not grasp why
Eddie treated me the way he did.

I took this recent letter as a threat; I was on the lookout,
hyper-vigilant to my surroundings. Here I have the eggers,
and now an anonymous letter. What next? Both of these
things made me feel really creepy, so I put a security system
in the house—more money I could not afford to spend.

I did bring the letter to the police department. I asked
to be assigned a detective; I felt like a puzzle. A puzzle sits

and waits to be put together to be made whole. I was not whole—I questioned my sanity so much. Was this all PTSD affecting me, or was this real fear?

My friends, family, counselor, and church are all concerned for all the harassments going on in my life. I am frightened, I am on edge. It just seems like I am paranoid at all things coming at me. Will someone hurt me, I wondered? I started checking around my car in the mornings and around the house.

I felt bad—one day poor Kevin went to go to throw something in the trash, which is right next to the back door. He reached his hand over and locked the door—he was protecting his family. We were all worried and scared.

Kay, being my best friend, had done some digging with a few of her friends. With all the court alienation and the hecklers accusing me of having a popular blog site, Kay did some sleuthing online to see whether they created a blog site for me; instead they found out that Vicky had a blog site! And it was dedicated to me! When I saw it I was appalled, sick, and angry. She was using Eddie's words to attack me— "cyber-bullying" by an adult, wow! I was amazed at all the wording. She wrote "It is all about you!"—Eddie's words; "to the psycho"—Eddie's words; "get over it!!!!"—Eddie's words' "she hates people who screw with others and she cannot wait to go to see Jimmy Buffet." All the writings had lots of exclamation marks just like that anonymous letter. The verbiage was the same on the blog as on the letter!

I could not believe the high school mentality. Oh, my God! If she only could have lived in my shoes! I thought, she seems to be mean as he is; this is all so cruel. I felt like he really does believe I am crazy and has others convinced that I am! I ask myself, how does a crazy person hold down a

job, run a house, keep food on the table, go to church, go to
college, and keep the kids medical needs up to par. I keep
asking myself, "What is wrong with this picture?

The blog site continued to leave messages about truth,
and how things are always someone else's fault; how some
people hate the world and are miserable; calling some people
liars; and that the truth will come out. People will eventually
unravel when they lose control. I thought, she is Eddie.

I always ran to Bobbie at the Battered Women's Shelter
when Eddie was hurting me, or when I felt violated. She told
me that an abuser will get a campaign of friends and people
to gang up against the victim. I never thought this would happen to me. Bobbie also told me that if a man or a partner talks
bad about his ex—then run. Vicky has no idea! I wished she
had a heart. She got the prize all right—the booby prize. She
does not even know! Or I wondered, is she an abuser also?
Emily said she is not even nice to her own daughter. So hey—
maybe I see harassment here—cyber-harassment; but how
can one prove it is me she is talking about? She did not use
my name. I know in my heart of hearts it is me.

I called my lawyer about the blog site Vicky set up, and
I told him this Web site made me feel uneasy, and that I was
on guard for my safety. I told him about being vandalized
and about the anonymous letter. He said, "Nothing is prov-
able—it is all circumstantial." But it all fits and points to the
guilty party or parties!

How childish are these accusations? This is childish, but
I felt violated and on guard. How many girlfriends in this
country kill for their boyfriends? I feel this especially now,
since I can see into her mind with the Web blog; what she
thinks of me is so untrue.

My feelings are that Vicky must think that Eddie's family

agrees with her. It has to be me, Amy. I thought—no, Miss Vicky, you have no idea how they treated me. I thought— he is Mommy's baby and he can do no wrong. The whole family put him on a pedestal, oh, and especially now that he is a real fireman. I feel he hides behind being a hero fireman; I thought, why would he ever have hurt his wife and children? Now would he?

The detective came to my home and I told him everything. He said, "I checked out your police reports before I came here." He suggested that I install a night camera and other preventions. He said he had not a doubt in his mind who was doing this to me, and that he would be the first to cuff the offenders and bring them in, but we had to catch them in the act. He was a wonderful man and truly caring and compassionate to my concerns.

At this point, I will do anything to make this harassment stop before someone gets hurt, mainly me! Both my lawyer and the detective are saying there is nothing I can do unless I catch them. There should be some kind of law against this. I have been vandalized for almost a year and a half!!

The children have said this to me: "Mom, Vicky's camp is right on the way, she could be doing this on the Friday nights as she goes to her camp and drives right by here!" Even the kids are figuring this out! I was protecting my property and whole self now! It just seems like Eddie's world is out to get me, and I have had enough—I want peace!

I talked to the mayor's secretary, Monique. She had called me to ask about some BOSE speakers I had donated to city hall. We had previously struck up a good relationship when I worked at BOSE; I helped her husband get a job there during our holiday season. Well, she could not find out where the speakers had gone; they were trying to account for all inventory, and she remembered I had donated enough speakers to make city hall have the better sound that it needed, since the PA system there sucked. I told her the previous mayor did not want them and so the vet's center took them. But I was not sure if they used them or not. We talked about our lives a bit, and I told her some of what was happening in my life—with the divorce, abuse, alienation, and now the fear for my life. She knew me pretty well, and she encouraged me to talk to our new mayor; he would not like this one bit.

She said something that really stuck with me. She said, "Amy, everyone has a right to a free life—freedom to live peacefully. This is not right."

I told her, "I will think about it."

I was afraid to talk to the mayor; I was afraid he, too, would think I was crazy. I was afraid of Eddie. I thought long and hard about taking the trip to see the mayor of our town. I called and made an appointment. I had told my pastor, and my new counselor, Dr. Sam, that I was going to do this. I thought to myself: they probably think I am off my rocker. But I had enough of this; I was at war. The children were having PTSD symptoms, they were looking for henchmen hired by eggers casing our house! This is beyond enough!

I prepared myself the day before: I had all my evidence, police reports, blog site copies, anonymous letter, DSS reports stating they support a child abuse claim—a 51A against Eddie, DSS reports that SOMEONE called on me unsupported accusations, porno bills showing the mindset of this type of ill man, and the interrogatories.

I brought everything I had, not to start trouble, but to stop trouble and prevent me from ending up dead. A lot of the vandalisms took place near court dates—I had compared the dates. Also, on band night, pink paintballs hit my car while he had the children and I was home alone. Too many things added up pointing to the guilty parties.

I showed up at the mayor's office that morning and waited for an hour to see him; he had been running late. I sat down calmly; I had my agenda ready with what I needed to show him and discuss with him. I am a businesswoman, so I had everything in order to present to him.

Well, when I showed him everything, he looked upset and said, "This is stalking! Plain and simple, this is not going to be allowed in my town."

I knew he genuinely cared about what I was saying, and he cared about the children. I had tears in my eyes as he listened to me. I was happy—he was going to help me.

Then he said, "Are you getting help?"

I said, "Yes, I am. It has been a hard road."

He said, "If anything comes up, you go see Detective Saget. He will be on your case; I will take care of this."

I left him copies of all the evidence, and I thanked him. I left his office knowing I did the right thing. I swear, God guided me though that meeting. I felt at ease. The mayor is a good man; he is a just man. Fireman or not, the mayor will get to the bottom of this; he made me feel safer.

A funny thing happened the next day. I went out to my car and looked at the window that always got bombed, and down below was one lone egg. It was placed neatly on the ground at the bottom of the window that is usually bombed. Imagine that! The eggers came and did not make a sound. Now why would they do that? To let me know they can get me anytime? That they are still here no matter what, or will they wait for time to go by? Will they do something more outlandish and childish, or will they really hurt someone?

CHAPTER 11
Dr. SAM

After talking to the mayor, I felt like a big weight was lifted off my shoulders. My lawyer had filed interrogatories to question Eddie about the vandalisms and the anonymous letter. Funny thing—Eddie said, "Do you really think we are that immature?" I wanted to laugh! Poor guy has no idea! I thought, he really does not know how Vicky acts, but his children do. Why on earth can't men listen to their children? Kids instinctively know when someone is not good, and they will love unconditionally when someone is kind and good.

I had started seeing Dr. Sam; she is a certified trauma councilor. She studied under a trauma doctor, who is actually located in Boston; I felt that my faith had led me to Dr. Sam. It could only be that God intervened, for me to end up with the best trauma specialist around. My other counselor who had diagnosed me with PTSD had had a heart attack and was no longer practicing, and Dr. Tim could not help me—there were too many other dynamics there. But I found Dr. Sam; she is a kind and petite woman with a very gentle demeanor.

I was falling apart in her office. When I first arrived I was scared, paranoid, hyper-vigilant, and jumpy. I felt so alone and under attack. I was at war, fighting for my sanity and for my children's. I had an overwhelming sense of injustice and a strong desire to do something about it; I needed my say, and I needed help! I had all the PTSD symptoms going on: worry, doubt, and fear of everything: real fear, and irrational fear. Eddie was my trigger; I could not go near him. I could not breathe, even when I was talking about him. I was frightened, and his crazy-making ways made me feel insane.

Dr. Sam put me at ease. She said, "Yes, you have PTSD, and together we will work through it." She is there for the long haul for me; I knew she would help me understand and help me to get to a point in which I am able to manage this disorder. I also needed to clear Eddie out of my life; with all the legal matters he was putting me through, as best I could. But in my heart, I know he will never stop attacking me, till he squishes me like a bug.

I did feel somewhat calmer after the DSS case: the children won their rights to choose whether they want to go with Eddie or not. I do have to say, "The children won that deal."

When I pulled the DSS records for court, there was an additional 51A marked "unsupported and closed." It named me as the perpetrator; as I read what the paperwork said, I was amazed that someone I thought was from Eddie's camp went as far as claiming I was a verbal abuser to the children.

The report stated, "The mother was not allowing the children to visit their father, and the mother yells at the children when they have visits with their father. The mother is a verbal abuser. Emily misses school often, though she has physician's notes." This was as if to claim I let her miss school just to miss school. The caller went on and on.

The DSS investigated and found nothing; they closed the case. This call was made before Eddie hit Kevin, while the alienation charges were going on. Can you imagine a person who would think of ways to get another person's children taken away? What kind of person does this? Someone very vengeful! SOMEONE was setting me up! I truly believe when someone calls the DSS, they should be accountable for their statements. I would have loved to stand before my accuser! I am sure they did not plan on receiving a supported 51A against Eddie.

The call was placed during the time of a fifteen-year-old daughter's life when mom is not their friend. Kids of this age group think they are the slaves and that they have to do everything in the house. What they really want is to find their own way and be independent from Mom. This is a natural process in a teenage girl's life. Looks like someone was looking for something on me again! Emily has health issues; she has chronic mono, chronic fatigue syndrome, and allergies that kick her immune system during every fall. As I told the mayor, "This is sad, that someone had to stoop that low to try and make me lose my children."

I am on guard. I do not trust what they will do next! Dr. Sam keeps me calm and we talk about the issues; we deal with everything moment by moment—it is a never ending roller coaster ride.

I still had to deal with Eddie about the tax issues. It was pitiful what happened with all that tax mess. His third lawyer won that round, guess why? Because his second lawyer had to put the case off three times due to his wife's illness and ultimate death. As a professional courtesy, my lawyer and I allowed that. So, we looked as if we had filed three frivolous contempt charges, when actually what happened was we had a heart for lawyer number two's family circumstances. Eddie and his new lawyer number three twisted that to their benefit. He owed me taxes from our divorce year, period!

The next year, when I filed as a single woman, the IRS grabbed my return to pay for Eddie's previous deficit. The amount was about the same as the money owed—$3,000. When we went to court, he then claimed he had already paid me the money, but what he did was twist it all to his benefit. He claimed that he did pay me back the year of my single-one tax return, and that he owed me nothing. In reality, he never paid me anything from the tax return during the year of the divorce. He showed the canceled check and the, "I am sorry" note.

During the year of the divorce's tax return, I worked all year, took the maximum taxes out, paid all the house taxes, kids—you name it. He paid nothing on his business taxes except at year end, and yet, I, in the end, suffered for that. I did not get my fair share of any return during the divorce year! We were not even living in the same house during that whole tax year! Talk about PTSD and feeling unjustified! How does Eddie always get away with crap? He used crazy-making in the court! The judge thinks he already paid me for that divorce year and that I filed three frivolous contempt charges. It was unbelievable! I had accountants verify this, and even his own accountant did so! But the way they presented and confused even the judge with their crazy-making was unbelievable.

My lawyer never wants to deal with Eddie again; I am not even sure he would take another case against Eddie. My lawyer has had enough of the circus ride also. And talk about a circus…when I was leaving the courtroom, I was feeling very sick to my stomach and had to get the hell out of there. I had to make my way through an isle of people who would not move their feet. As I was exiting, the guard in the court started screaming at me to get out of the courtroom. Something had happened! I thought someone had gotten shot—it was like something out of a movie; he scared the crap out of me. I looked at Gracie when we got outside the door and asked what had happened. Gracie said my purse brushed up against Vicky and she started screaming ASSAULT! I wanted to faint. Oh, my God! I did not even know or feel anything.

I thought to myself, she made up that drama herself! I in no way did that intentionally to her. I did not even notice she was there! I was too worried I was going to trip on those people who would not move their feet. I was sick and my lawyer said, "Go home." I thought to myself, that would seem to fit her MO to get me like that. I told Gracie I needed to go see Pastor and pray. And that is just what I did. Pastor and I talked about it, and I cried and cried: "What more can happen with these people before I am dead! They are trying to make me look like a monster of some type!" Pastor told me to write her a quick note and apologize to her and tell her the truth, even if she caused her own drama.

I did. I wrote Vicky a note and sent it by registered mail. She never filed charges; I had many other things to counter-file. I even went to the courthouse with all my evidence; I had enough to file a restraining order. The women at the filing office at the courthouse encouraged me to file because I did fear for my life. What could be next! I thought long and hard and knew I did not want another court case. I am in debt so badly; I am not sure I will ever get out of it due to all the legal fees I have endured.

I ended up dropping the appeal for the tax issue, even though another well-known state rep, who is always for the underdog, said he would help and probably win, but it would cost me more to fight it. I counseled with him, Dr. Sam, and my pastors; emotionally and financially I could not handle anymore of Eddie's insanity. I dropped the case. I always felt ripped off by this guy financially, but in the heart of the matter, I won. I let it go! Better to be wronged sometimes.

I felt like another weight was lifted off my shoulders. I needed to let it go. He had nothing else to come and get me about—for now, I thought.

But I was on alert to what could be next. What were they planning next? I wondered, is it the PTSD causing me to be on alert, or was it my gut that knew he was never going to stop?

The ball did drop, and my lawyer called, and Eddie filed for court fees on the tax issue and won. I bet he felt like a real winner. I really think that judge hates women! I have heard that same thing from many other women throughout my church community. In my jurisdiction you have to have the same judge for the rest of your life when going back to family court, and that type of law sucks! I feel so much injustice has taken place over the years with Eddie… I cry for it just to end. I had to let it go.

Dr. Sam helped me understand that I had trauma growing up, as well as the car accidents afterward, but the icing

on the cake was Eddie. He did me in and the marriage did
me in; I cannot let the divorce and its ending do me in. I was
so on edge, I felt like giving up many times, like just driving
my car into a bridge. I could not give up on my children—
they meant everything to me and I know God had plans for
them and for me. The verse in *The New King James Bible*,
Jeremiah 29:11 says:

"For I know the thoughts that I think toward you, says
the Lord, thoughts of peace and not of evil, to give you a
future and a hope."

This Bible verse saved me. Many times driving home
from work, I cried out to the Lord, and I cried many, many
tears before I got home, so the children would not see me. I
screamed, "Lord help me. I know I have a future and a path,
and I know you have a plan for me. I will follow you always.
He wants me to have peace! God never abandons us. We are
his children. He protects us and loves us, just as I do my
own flesh-and- blood children. I will always be there for
them, always.

With Post Traumatic Stress Disorder, I felt numb. It is
the weirdest feeling. I sometimes think about *The Wizard of
Oz*, when they are running through the poppy field and life
is good. They are all running to the light, and they see the
happiness of the Emerald City ahead. All of a sudden, they
all start dropping one by one. They stop dead in their tracks,
numb to life, numb to their feelings, with blank stares, as in
a coma-like state of shock, a dead sleep. But the Lion, Tin
Man, Scarecrow, Dorothy, and Toto do get saved—a certain
higher power saves them. It is a story true to real life; we can
save ourselves with good counsel and a higher power. Mine
are God and Dr. Sam; they are the maintenance for life.

I remember a statement Eddie said to me during the verbal assault on band night. He shook his head and said, "I do not know how you are keeping this all up!" He looked around my little kitchen, and at the boys.

I still reflect on these words: is it because I have *not* lost it? Or is it because he can*not* break me? I wonder which one it is.

I remember those words he said when he left: "By the time I am through with you, you will have no house, no car, no kids, no nothing."

I think about both those statements: one when he left, and one when I knew I would never speak to him again in my life.

I don't have "our" house, I have my own. I don't have "our" car, I have my own. I have my children and I have their love and their respect. I still have some trouble relating to my own self-worth, but I am getting stronger, and I definitely have a hope and a future.

I remember hearing a tune in my head one morning in the shower before church. Was God telling me something? I could hear this tune, but could not remember the song. I went to church and Pastor spoke about forgiveness that morning. As I drove home I kept hearing the same tune and then the words, "It's about forgiveness..." I said to myself: I know that song, but from where? I got home and got lunch ready for the kids and then all of a sudden I knew right where to find it.

With that inner spirit thing coming through me, I went to my DVD collection and picked up the Eagles DVD, "When Hell Freezes Over"—isn't that fitting. I put the DVD on and went right to that song, "The Heart of the

Matter." I stood there with tears rolling down my face and hearing these words:

"I've been trying to get down to the heart of the matter but my will gets weak and my thoughts seam to scatter. But I think it's about forgiveness…..forgiveness"

At that moment I knew I had forgiven Eddie for all he had done. I had loved him for a time—maybe for the wrong reasons—but I had truly forgiven him.

I still know my boundaries. Between Dr. Sam and Bobbie I will always have boundaries from bullies in this world. I will never be able to speak to or be near Eddie again in my life. I am at peace with that decision—I will always fear him.

Because I have PTSD does not mean that I am crazy; it just means I have had a life-altering experience or experiences. I know my triggers—what makes me feel uncomfortable: triggers of abuse, loud noises, bullies, crazy-making people, relationships, trusting, being on guard, and waiting for what is next.

I remember who I was before—never on edge. Where did I go? I am still here. I know it, I can feel me. I can smile.

I am learning to be me again. Dr. Sam is teaching me one day at a time, and it is a never ending road.

CHAPTER 12
AN OPEN LETTER

Recently, I was working a fundraiser for our local veterans' organization, and the mayor came up to me and said, "Hi, Amy. How are things going for you?"

I said, "Mr. Mayor, things are great. I have had no incidents at all! I do not know what you did, but I want to thank you."

The mayor said, "No one messes with the lives of children. I am happy to hear this; all is good."

Just that short conversation made a difference, knowing he did do something. I thought to myself, he must have pulled Eddie onto the carpet and told him something like: "If I find out you have anything to do with this, you will lose your job. Or, "This is serious—you better think about it; stalking and vandalism could mean jail time, if you are caught." Then I bet Eddie went right to Vicky and told her what the mayor said.

I can only imagine, if Eddie has no idea about any of this, I think she does. Every hint of vandalism has stopped, but I still fear for my life, and I always look around when I go out to my car. I look around to see if my home has any damage to it. Or is there someone down the street, ready to shoot me? I think if she is anything like him, she may plan to get me one day. Is that real fear or irrational fear? I believe that it is real fear. I am not crazy. This I now know.

Having Post Traumatic Stress Disorder, or knowing and loving someone who does, certainly does not mean they are crazy. Please understand that for your own sake, and for the sake of your loved ones. Having PTSD means you have been wounded, and your life has been altered in some unmistakable way.

Rightfully so, I found out just what it feels like to be wounded through the trauma. I also know what it feels like to be made fun of by the one who was supposed to love, honor, and cherish me all the days of my life; that is the "ultimate betrayal." I have been called names by a family member and by so-called friends—maybe those were never my friends. In fact, I now call them fair-weather friends— ones who had addictions to hide their own pain. I had joined them by hiding my own pain, at one point in time. I had finally reached a point where I did not want to hide my pain anymore—I wanted to be happy, peaceful, and to find my purpose. I wanted freedom from the chains I had been dragging around with me.

Hell knocked on my door one day at a Jimmy Buffet concert. Like a shutter on a camera, the pictures can be taken so fast you cannot see the true picture—just a jumbled mess of blur and confusion—a flashback of many traumas jumbled together: being bothered by loud sounds and star-tling effects, feeling alone and helpless, feeling on alert, and feeling threatened.

I have never felt like that in my life; the effects lasted for months. Looking back, I can see that God was good to me. He pulled me out of a bad marriage before I died in that prison of misery.

I pray that in your reading of this book, you will better understand that anyone can have PTSD. Post Traumatic Stress Disorder does not discriminate between gender, race, or age. I have wondered: how can I have a disorder like a veteran? They have seen such horrible things—dismembered friends, death, fear, the sounds of gun fire, bombs, and screaming. I can *FEEL* what they feel and I *CRY* with them. I *CRY* for the 9/11 and Katrina survivors—I have heard and read their stories. I cry for *ANYONE* who has had to suffer through shock, devasta-tion, and loss. At first, PTSD can come in small waves the way mine did, and then BOOM!—a bully with the traits of an emotional abuser ends up being my husband. Who would have thought that my marriage to this guy would spark off this kind of explosion of my life?

In my opinion, as time goes by, PTSD will be rampant in this world. Where war, violence, earthquakes, hurricanes, and all life-altering situations exist, PTSD is there. People need to talk about this disorder. They need to understand it, recognize it, and do something about it.

I know that so many vets commit suicide because they cannot live with the nightmares, the sounds, the smells, the helpless feelings. They ask themselves so many questions: What is life all for? Why am I here? What is my purpose? Who will ever want me now that I am wounded? Does any one understand me? I cannot concentrate at work or do anything! What good am I? Shall I just drown myself in alcohol or drugs? I could just leave—no one would miss me, right? I have so much fear; is it real? When will the fear stop? Could it be when heaven calls my name? I need my say; why can't anyone hear me? I cannot stop my thinking in my head... Please, someone understand and help! I feel numb! I feel dead!

These are the same questions and thoughts *every* PTSD victim asks himself or herself. Over and over again: how can I make this all STOP?

I went to a funeral for a veteran friend of mine. His daughter gave a beautiful eulogy to her dad, and she ended it with "The demons got the best of my dad." He died on his birthday, Independence Day. How terribly sad and what a complete loss! He was an awesome man who was full of spunk, and he always fought for justice. I wish I could have known how to help—he also had PTSD. We were both fighting the same war in our minds. I loved him like a brother.

He died during the beginning of my divorce, at just the moment in time when I was in no shape to reach out; I could not even help myself then. I have such a need to connect with others like me because we can understand each other. I have another vet friend; I actually call him my best buddy. He too has PTSD and he acts just like me—it's odd. We kind of laugh with each other about all the irrational fears we have. We joke around about our eccentricities and blame it on PTSD. I do not know the cause or details of his trauma, and he does not know mine, but we relate, we can be ourselves, and feel accepted with our human illness. How freeing.

I also have spoken about PTSD in my book-writing class at college; people come to me after class telling me their own stories of PTSD. They tell me with tears in their eyes. I want to hug them and tell them everything will be okay. It will never be okay again, since they will always have those memories. But they will learn what triggers their reactions to those memories and learn to adjust day by day, one day at a time.

I feel like I am one of the lucky ones; I am learning how to live with PTSD and I am living differently than I used to. I avoid what triggers me, like bullies, people who manipulate others, and any hostile environment. Most PTSD people avoid what triggers them. Both the mind and the heart are fragile. When wounded inside, we need a hand, a prayer, someone to listen to what we cannot understand. I had to find God and thankfully, he has done most of that for me. He has put all the right people in my path to set me in the right direction for peace, solace, and healing.

I hope you have gained insight into my purpose for writing this book: to open your eyes and hearts to all wounded human beings.

My additional hope is for people with Post Traumatic Stress Disorder—PLEASE seek the help, and the love, and the understanding you do need, to live.

"Ask, and it will be given to you; seek, and you will find; knock, and it will be opened to you. For everyone who asks receives, and he who seeks finds, and to him who knocks it will be open." (Matthew 7:7- 8, *The New King James Bible*)

REFLECTIONS and RESOURCES
SCREAMING SILENTLY;
WAGES OF WAR IN A SOUND MIND

Post Traumatic Stress Disorder, or PTSD, involves the human mind and the central nervous system. PTSD is common in all veterans of war and other related life-threatening occurrences in the secular population. PTSD invades the mind and the five senses. According to the National Center for PTSD at the U.S. Department of Veteran Affairs, "the condition is associated with a number of neurological and physiological changes." A perfect description of PTSD from the Vietnam Veterans of America is,

"PTSD is the normal reaction of a normal person to abnormal circumstances."

Being a veteran of war or a victim of violent crimes, natural disasters, terrorism, emotional or physical abuse—these all are considered life-threatening or life-altering traumas.

When people think of PTSD, they think of Vietnam veterans or veterans of war. Some victims know they have it, and some have no idea what is wrong with them. It is a silent haunting. The ones who do not know they have this problem have masked the disorder with other substances, such as abusing drugs and alcohol, or they have isolated themselves from people, including family. There is numbness in the mind and body; it is almost like going into shock and never coming out of it. Imagine being so frightened and horrified that your mind snaps and your system goes into auto-pilot mode.

A Vietnam veteran told me a story about an incident he had in Vietnam, and the expression on his face also told the story in painful detail. He told me his unit had "dug in," as it is called. During wars, soldiers dug holes in the ground. He was in his foxhole; he could hear and smell all the firearms and explosions all around him. All of a sudden, he felt something hit him near his stomach. He looked down to see a grenade. Fear and instinct took over; he grabbed the grenade and threw it out of the foxhole, only to hear and see it explode; it went up and out. He prayed to God for saving his life at that moment. Then again, another grenade landed, thump, right on his lap. His thoughts were: how could this happen again? This is a nightmare! This is not happening. Again he picked it up to push it out of the foxhole, only for it to blow up more quickly than had the last one. This one sparked pain in his legs. Scraps of metal became imbedded and the pain was horrific. Then there were more explosions around him, dirt was flying everywhere, there were sounds of thunder, and the earth rumbled. They were close! The enemy was close and he was scared to death! He prayed, he cried, and he came home wounded. This resulted in Post Traumatic Stress Disorder. Is this a "normal reaction of a normal person to abnormal circumstances"?

He did not ask for a mental health issue, but he received it. The National Vietnam Veterans Readjustment Study (NVVRS) found a lifetime PTSD rate of 67% among combat-wounded veterans (Kulka et al.,1990; EBSCO Host p. 69).

"There are both neurological and physiological changes that are associated with PTSD. PTSD alters both the central and autonomic nervous system. It affects the processing and integration of memory and also coordination of the body's fear response. The physiological effects include hyper-arousal in the sympathetic nervous system, increased startle reflex and disrupted sleep patterns" (National Center for PTSD US Department of Veteran Affairs).

Also, the repercussions of PTSD in daily lives can become chronic and interfere with the quality of life. This includes always being on guard, or experiencing a startling response to: the loud bangs of daily life, a door slamming, a car backfiring, a dish falling, an explosive thunderstorm, and feet stomping across the floor. The environment must be quiet and peaceful in order to avoid reacting to things in an out-of-control manner.

There can be lots of anger in the traumatized person. They just want it to stop, stop feeling like, "What is next"? Yes, they can hear a pin drop, or a potato chip fall on the floor across the room. Always on guard. Sometimes sadness and depression fill their lives.

When the vets from Iraq come home, they should seek help even if they think they are okay. Awareness of PTSD can keep the disorder from festering into something that could get out of control and affect their total being and their relationships. Families need to learn how to help, to be aware of

PTSD and the signs. They should assure the veteran they are not the enemy.

We also have accident victims who suffer from PTSD. As in the case of the veteran, circumstances happen to accident victims that can be mind altering. The victim fears for his or her life

I will use myself as a prime example: I was driving my sports car, passing a semi-truck when the truck came into my lane and hit my car. The car spun out of control, hitting the truck. I was pushed some fifty feet in front of the truck; I went into a 360° spin, and then a 180° spin. It all happened so fast. Within the few moments that it took place, I saw my vehicle going under the truckers' rig, and I passed out from fear—only to wake and see trees coming at me. I hit the brakes so hard my hip came out of its socket. The sounds of crashing metal echoed in my mind.

"Am I still alive?" I asked myself. In shock, cold and shaken, I was found—still alive. The experience was somewhat like being in a ride called the Tilt a Whirl at an amusement park. The ride just spins and spins, yet also gives the feeling like you're on the Whip, whipping back and forth. The natural instinct is to get out and get away in order to avoid the fear that sets in, as well as the shock and awe.

The same is true for horrific natural disasters, such as Hurricane Katrina for example. "Rates of serious mental disorders, including depression and PTSD doubled among survivors in Alabama, Louisiana, and Mississippi." (ESBCO *Science News*).

The memories of a disaster such as this will be numbing—the sounds of wind whipping, flying objects banging, glass breaking. When it is over, what are the damages? No roofs, flooding, loved ones missing, no home, no bed, no food, shock and awe.

According to "Natural Disasters & PTSD," "Most victims feel a number of emotions ranging from numbness to anger. They feel disoriented and guilty for having survived when others did not. Studies show one in four people developed PTSD after a major disaster" (Lee/Lee). Katrina was a monster, and the people of New Orleans have had life-threatening, mind-altering experiences. We have yet to do all that is humanly possible for Katrina survivors. Yet they are normal people living through an abnormal circumstance.

As a nation, we watched a terrorism attack on our country on September 11, 2001. What trauma we as a nation endured, but what about the trauma that occurred for the responders and the survivors? People ran for their lives; they literally ran out of their shoes from FEAR. Shoes were scattered everywhere. Imagine being that scared? Survivors were greeted by blood and body parts when exiting the towers. People were jumping out of the towers to their deaths. The noises from the planes, noises from shattering glass and debris were falling on them and all around them. Talk about shock and awe, these are traumatized people. They live with PTSD. Are they crazy? No. "PTSD is the normal reaction of a normal person to abnormal circumstances." These were definitely abnormal circumstances. This was a major attack, a life- threatening scenario.

Abuse, whether physical or emotional, can cause PTSD. In relationships, this could be the worst torment of them all. Here you are, involved with someone who professes to love you, yet he belittles your mind, body, and soul. Physical damage scars go away, but emotional scars do not.

"An abuser is a predator, a bully, a minimizer, someone who forms vulgar words, making the victim feel crazy. What is next? Always on edge and afraid. Then the abuse comes. Are you ready? Or is it again shock and awe and the victim is caught off guard?

"Secrecy and silence are the perpetrator's first line of defense. If secrecy fails, the perpetrator attacks the creditability of his victim. If he cannot silence her absolutely, he tries to make sure no one listens. To this end, he marshals an impressive array of arguments, from the most blatant denial to the most sophisticated and elegant rationalization. After every atrocity one can expect to hear the same predictable apologies: it never happened; the victim lies, the victim exaggerates, the victim brought it upon herself, and in any case it is time to forget the past and move on. The more powerful the perpetrator, the greater is his prerogative to name and define reality, and the more completely his arguments prevail" (*Trauma and Recovery*, Herman p. 8).

This passage shows the GREATEST kind of crazy-making, in which the abuser dismisses everything about a human life. It is sick and sad. This type of abuse is mind-blowing. The victim does not know who she/he is; the victim is confused and numb. Every time the abuser twists words and thoughts to make them even uglier for the victim, the numbness of what is reality sets in for the victim. PTSD is inevitable: fight or flight. Here you have a normal person, in the midst of an abnormal circumstance.

This is also the same form of abuse used in concentration camps. The POW might have his arm broken, and the abuser might say it is all in your head and to quit whining. Then the victim is ignored. If any officials come and look at the broken arm, the abuser would say that it must have just happened. That is what bullies did on the playground in our childhood.

The movies, in many ways, show these types of mental head games, from Abbott and Costello, making light and being funny about it and causing much confusion, to some of the modern-day dramas, in which the hero saves the victim. In real life, no one saves the victim but the victim. With proper help and counseling, the affects of PTSD will quiet down. Being a person with PTSD is like being an alcoholic: it will be a lifetime of work. The victim learns what triggers them and thus works on correcting the mind set of the trauma.

Whether a veteran of war, a person who is emotionally tormented and abused, or a victim of a natural disaster, whether it be a hurricane, an earthquake, terrorism, or a car accident, fear is the culprit. Fear of death, fear of fright, fear of bodily harm, fear of not feeling anything, fear of confusion, fear of the unknown. When will fear strike again?

The mind does the same dance in all the circumstances described. We have very different circumstances but the same mental warfare. The symptoms are the same, the name is the same, and the people are the same. Yes, all life-threatening traumas are equally traumatic to the human mind. Chemically and psychologically they are same.

The King James Bible states in 2 Timothy 1:7:

"For God hath not given us the spirit of fear; but of power, and of love, and a sound mind."

Even in the Bible we can learn that we were all created with a sound mind. Fear was not given to us. Does this scripture give a person with PTSD hope of healing? Yes, it does, through faith.

Dr. Joel O.Brende, M.D. and J. Keith Miller have different twelve- step programs that invite God to help with the recovery process. Just as an alcoholic has a twelve-step program, so does PTSD. There is healing and it takes work—a lifetime of work and help. The wounded just need to reach out. Healing also comes from a community and awareness of the problem.

The Signs of PTSD

Hyper-arousal   Social Withdrawal
Startle Effect   Impaired Work Performance
Insomnia   Distrust
Fatigue Exhaustion   Feeling Abandoned
Interpersonal Symptoms   Feeling Rejected
Headaches   Over protectiveness
Vulnerability to Illness   Feeling Numb
Reactive Depression   Always on Guard

Cognitive Effects

Impaired Concentration   Decreased Self-Esteem
Memory Impairment   Intrusive thoughts & Memories
Worry   Spacey Feeling, Zombie State
Disassociation   Feelings of Detachment
Avoidance of anything that reminds you of the Trauma.
An overwhelming sense of Injustice & a strong desire to do something about it.

WORKS CITED

Bower, Bruce. "Katrina's Two-Sided News Impact," EBSCO HOST. Science News 2006.

Dikel, Engdahl, and Eberly. "PTSD in Former Prisoners of War: Prewar, Wartime, and Postwar Factors," EBSCO HOST. International Society for Traumatic Stress Studies. *Journal Of Traumatic Stress*, Volume 18, Issue 1, 2005.

Evans, Patricia. *The Verbally Abusive Relationship*, 2nd ed. Avon, Mass.: Adams Media, 1996.

Henley, Don, with Souther, J.D. The Eagles: "When Hell Freezes Over; "The Heart of the Matter." 1994 Deffen Records, Inc., Image Entertainment, Inc.

Herman, Judith Lewis, M.D.. *Trauma and Recovery*. USA: Basic Books, 1992, p. 8.

King James Bible. USA: World Bible Publishers 243AB, 2 Timothy 1:7.

Lee, Mary Price and Richard S. Lee. *Natural Disasters and PTSD*. New York: The Rosen Publishing Group, 1996, p.54.

The National Vietnam Veterans Readjustment Study NVVRS: http://www.va.gov/

New King James Bible. Nashville, TN: Thomas Nelson Bibles, 1982, Jeremiah 29:11.

United States Department of Veteran Affairs/ National Center for PTSD pg. 1-4. www.ncptsd.va.gov/facts

Vietnam Veterans of America VVAPTSD/Substance Abuse Committee 2004 Flyer.

RESOURCES

Books

Trauma and Recovery, by Judith Lewis Herman.M.D.
Waking the Tiger, by Peter Levine
Failure to Scream, by Robert Hicks
Blinded by Love, by Monique Houde
The Verbally Abusive Relationship, by Patricia Evans
The Emotionally Abusive Relationship, by Beverly Engel
No Visible Wounds Mary, by Susan Miller, PhD
Hunger for Healing, by J. Keith Miller
Changes That Heal, by Dr. Henry Cloud
Boundaries: When to Say Yes, When to Say No, to Take Control of Your Life by Henry Cloud and Dr. John Townsend

Web Sites

National Center for PTSD
http://www.ncptsd.va.gov/ncmain/information/

Gateway to PTSD Information
http://www.ptsdinfo.org/

Monique Houde
www.choices4tomorrow.com

National Domestic Violence Hotline 800-799-SAFE
http://www.ndvh.org/

Battered Women's Resources Northeast USA
http://www.bwri.com/news.htm

Kathie Costos
http://www.namguardianangel.org/

http://www.bullyonline.org/stress/ptsd.htm